TEMPEST V
vs
Fw 190D-9

1944–45

ROBERT FORSYTH

OSPREY PUBLISHING
Bloomsbury Publishing Plc
PO Box 883, Oxford, OX1 9PL, UK
1385 Broadway, 5th Floor, New York, NY 10018, USA
E-mail: info@ospreypublishing.com
www.ospreypublishing.com

OSPREY is a trademark of Osprey Publishing Ltd

First published in Great Britain in 2019

A catalogue record for this book is available from the British Library.

ISBN: PB 9781472829252; eBook 9781472829269; ePDF 9781472829276;
XML 9781472829283

19 20 21 22 23   10 9 8 7 6 5 4 3 2 1

Edited by Tony Holmes
Cover artwork and battlescene by Gareth Hector
Three-views, cockpits, Engaging the Enemy and armament scrap views by Jim
Laurier
Maps and formation diagrams by Bounford.com
Index by Alan Rutter
Typeset by PDQ Digital Media Solutions, Bungay, UK
Printed in China through World Print Ltd.

Osprey Publishing supports the Woodland Trust, the UK's leading woodland
conservation charity.

To find out more about our authors and books visit **www.ospreypublishing.com**.
Here you will find extracts, author interviews, details of forthcoming events and
the option to sign up for our newsletter.

Acknowledgements

I am grateful to former Fw 190D-9 pilot Gerhard H. Kroll, who I met in the
USA back in 1990 and with whom I corresponded extensively, and to Dr.
James H. Kitchens III. I would also like to express my particular thanks to
Chris Thomas for his guidance, suggestions and assistance with photographs
and also to Eddie J. Creek for similar help as always. My thanks also to Nick
Beale, Donald Caldwell, Tony Holmes, Nick Stroud, John Weal and *The
Aviation Historian* for their kind contributions to this book. The magnificent
works of Chris Thomas and Christopher Shores, of Jerry Crandall, of
J. Richard Smith and Eddie J. Creek and of Marc Deboeck, Eric Larger and
Tomás Poruba have all helped to make this book the more enjoyable to write
and they are recommended unreservedly to those seeking to learn more about
the two outstanding aeroplanes which this volume covers.

Dedication

This book is dedicated to James H. Kitchens, Christopher Shores and Manfred
Griehl – three aviation historians who, many years ago, said 'yes' when others
said 'no'.

Cover Art

Shortly after midday on 27 December 1944, a large *Gruppe*-sized formation of
around 40 Fw 190D-9s of III./JG 54 took off from their base at Varrelbusch,
in northern Germany, on a flight intended to offer airfield cover to Ar 234 jet
bombers based at Münster-Handorf and to help familiarise the unit's pilots –
many of whom were recently trained – with the Münster basin area. At
1250 hrs, having flown south in a staggered formation at between 6,500–
9,800ft in cloudless skies, the Focke-Wulfs were alerted by ground control to
the presence of eight enemy aircraft above them in the vicinity of Münster. It
would fall to the 12 Fw 190D-9s of the top-cover *Staffel*, flying about 1,650ft
above the rest of the formation, and led by Leutnant Peter Crump (one of the
more experienced of the German pilots airborne that day), to deal with the
enemy threat. Crump was probably flying his assigned Fw 190D-9 'White 16'.
The enemy comprised eight Tempest Vs of No. 486 Sqn RNZAF that had
sortied from B.80 Volkel, in Holland, on an armed reconnaissance patrol
initially bound for the Paderborn area until it was redirected to Münster. The
fighters were led by Sqn Ldr K. G. Taylor-Cannon, known to his comrades as
'Hyphen', who was flying EJ828/SA-Z. The Tempests swooped down on
Crump's *Staffel* from out of the sun. In the swirling mêlée that followed, JG 54
lost no fewer than six of its new fighters to the Tempests, four from Crump's
10. *Staffel* and two from 12. *Staffel*, the first to go down being 24-year-old
Oberleutnant Paul Breger of 10./JG 26, who bailed out of his 'Black 2'.
A few seconds later, Crump managed to wheel his Fw 190D-9 behind
Tempest EJ627/SA-E, flown by Flg Off Bevan Hall of No 486 Sqn's 'Green
Section' acting, as with Crump's aircraft, as top cover flight. Hall was pursuing
another aircraft of Crump's flight when he was in turn engaged by the pilot of
'Black 2'. Crump saw hits from his guns striking the enemy fighter, which
started to burn before pushing over into a dive, at which point the pilot bailed
out.

Any sense of elation Crump may have experienced at scoring his 21st
victory was quickly dashed when he saw Hall's now pilotless aircraft fly
straight into Breger's descending parachute, which began to catch fire. Breger
was killed when he came down near Telgte, to the east of Münster. Hall's
Tempest exploded when it hit the ground close to the road between Handorf
and Dorbaum. No. 486 Sqn claimed the destruction of four enemy aircraft,
including one Fw 190 that fell to Sqn Ldr Taylor-Cannon, whose Tempest is
portrayed on the cover of this book, along with the Fw 190D-9 of Leutnant
Crump, who claimed two Tempests shot down in total – the second fighter
was, in fact, only damaged. (Cover artworks by Gareth Hector)

Previous Page

No. 274 Sqn pilots in October 1944 at B.80 Volkel. In the centre front (with
his hands together) is Sqn Ldr J. R. Heap, who would be killed in a crash
following engine failure on take-off a few weeks later. At the far left of the
front row is Flt Lt D. C. 'Foob' Fairbanks, who would become the top-scoring
Tempest ace – possibly as many as six of his victories were Fw 190D-9s. He
later became CO of the squadron. Far right in the front row is Flt Lt R. B.
Cole, who would subsequently command No. 3 Sqn.

Contents

INTRODUCTION

It is a sad irony that war accelerates the pace of technological and mechanical advancement, and nowhere was this more the case than in military aviation during World War II.

In 1940, the British Swordfish torpedo-bomber, a biplane design which originated in the 1930s, gave a good account of itself in action against German U-boats, naval vessels and shipping, but in less than five years, by the summer of 1944, the RAF was deploying Meteor jet fighters against enemy V1 flying bombs over southern England. In Germany, likewise, the Luftwaffe continued to use the Hs 123 biplane dive-bomber and ground-attack aircraft that had first seen action in the Spanish Civil War through to 1945, by which point Me 262 and Ar 234 jet interceptors, bombers and reconnaissance aircraft were flying missions with frontline units.

Engine development also saw unprecedented movement in the early war years – as well as challenges. In Britain in December 1942, the motor engineering firm of D. Napier & Son was absorbed into the English Electric conglomerate and, under the supervision of former Royal Flying Corps (RFC) pilot Maj Frank Halford, it designed and produced a series of three 'H'-configured aero engines from 1930 that all differed in their four-stroke valve design. Named after bladed weapons, the series culminated in 1937 in the 24-cylinder water-cooled Sabre, which was developed to produce 3,000hp with skew gear-driven sleeve valves.

By 1941, the Napier Sabre had been earmarked for fitment into the planned Hawker Typhoon fighter, which was intended as a replacement for the Spitfire and Hurricane. However, problems dogged the programme early on, with unreliability manifesting itself in a lack of power on the part of the Sabre and manoeuvrability on the part of the Typhoon. Nevertheless, through a combination of accident, good and bad timing, luck, competition shortcomings and continuing enhancement, the

Sabre would ultimately prove itself in combat when fitted to what would become the Hawker Tempest V airframe.

In Germany, while Focke-Wulf's radial-engined Fw 190A series proved to be an outstanding companion to Messerschmitt's inline Bf 109, it was recognised that the Fw 190 lacked speed and manoeuvrability at high altitude. The aircraft was fitted with BMW 801 series engines, but as with the Sabre, there were problems which inhibited performance at height. Worse, nine early Fw 190A-0s and A-1s attached to a dedicated Luftwaffe test unit crashed in August–September 1941 and the finger of blame was pointed at BMW, whose engines continued to be plagued by overheating problems and compressor failures. There were also delays in deliveries of engines.

In late 1941 deliveries of the Fw 190A-2 began to reach *Jagdgeschwader* (JG) 26 on the Channel Front, this aircraft being fitted with an improved 1600hp BMW 801C-2 that included extra ventilation slots at the rear of the engine. However, as the war progressed, even with successive variants, BMW struggled to overcome restrictions in power. Fortunately, a potential solution was at hand in the Junkers Jumo 213A V12 liquid-cooled engine with a pressurized cooling system and single-stage, two-speed supercharging.

But none of this served to daunt two of the most creative, dedicated and driven aircraft designers and engineers who, in 1941, set about, separately, developing what would become two of the ultimate piston-engined fighters of the war.

Sydney Camm was born on 5 August 1893 in the Berkshire town of Windsor, to the west of London, the son of Fred, an accomplished carpenter and joiner, and

The rugged Tempest V became one of the best air superiority fighters of the war. This example, EJ705/W2-X, was assigned to 2nd TAF's No. 80 Sqn at B.80 Volkel, and bears the emblem of a kangaroo holding an Australian flag to signify its association with RAAF pilots serving with the unit. (CT Collection)

The Fw 190D-9 combined a sense of purpose with elegance. This factory-fresh production example, Wk-Nr.210051, was fitted with a 300-ltr drop tank and was bound for III./JG 54, the first Luftwaffe fighter unit to equip with the 'Dora' in September 1944. (EN-Archive)

his wife, Maria, and was the first born of twelve siblings (although only eleven lived). Five years later, nearly 900 miles away in the Prussian town of Bromberg, on 24 February 1898, Anna Tank gave birth to Kurt, a second child and only son for her and her husband Willi, a former sergeant in a grenadier regiment who worked as a maintenance technician and hydraulic engineer at an electrical powerplant.

Sydney left school at the age of 14 in 1908 and, following in the footsteps of his father, became an apprentice carpenter. Along with his brothers, he developed an interest in the cutting-edge science of aeronautics, and the Camm boys began to build high-quality model aircraft that they supplied to a local model shop in Eton. They soon realised that they could sell their models surreptitiously for higher prices to the boys of England's premier public school, Eton College, which they did by delivering them at night and tying them to string lowered from the windows of Eton's dormitories in order to avoid the wrath of the model shop's proprietors. Sydney and some friends also built a full-size, man-carrying glider, designed by Sydney, in a local council depot and they intended to power it with an engine. In 1912, Camm became a founding member of the local model aeroplane club.

In Prussia, at around the same time, young Kurt Tank aspired to fly, but on the outbreak of World War I, on the insistence of his father, rather than enrolling in the *Fliegertruppe* Kurt joined a cavalry regiment and was commissioned as a leutnant. By the end of that conflict he had been wounded on several occasions and had been cited for bravery.

In England, shortly after the commencement of the war, Sydney Camm had joined the Martinsyde Aircraft Company, based in sheds at the Brooklands motor-racing circuit in Weybridge, Surrey, initially as a carpenter. He was subsequently transferred to the drawing office, where he was employed for the remainder of the war.

During the interwar years, these two men worked to progress their careers in aviation design. Kurt Tank, who had become a qualified pilot, joined the Rohrbach Company in Berlin in the mid-1920s, where he was involved in flying boat design, but when that business started to experience financial difficulties he worked briefly for Messerschmitt in 1930–31 before joining Focke-Wulf in November 1931. Here, Tank worked on a wide range of cutting-edge designs such as the A 44/Fw 44, the Fw 56, Fw 58, Fw 187 and, in 1936, the majestic, four-engined Fw 200 Condor airliner for Lufthansa, which would eventually emerge as the Luftwaffe's main maritime strike aircraft.

In England in November 1923, Sydney Camm joined the Hawker Engineering Company, the successor to the Sopwith Aviation Company Ltd, as a Senior Draughtsman. During the late 1920s and early 1930s, Camm began to develop Hawker's metal build techniques, as well as fabric cover and metal designs such as in the Hawker Hart, Audax, Demon, Hind and Osprey. So successful were such designs and the faith that the RAF, Army and Fleet Air Arm had in them, that at one time during the 1930s, 84 per cent of the aircraft in the RAF were of Hawker/Camm design.

The outbreak of World War II would lend Tank's and Camm's designs even greater import. Tank's superb Fw 190 prototype had taken to the air for the first time from Focke-Wulf's plant at Bremen on 1 June 1939, while deliveries of a new Camm fighter, the Hawker Hurricane, were ramping up at the Kingston, Brooklands, Langley and Gloster Hucclecote factories. But not even Tank or Camm could have forecast just how much these basic designs – at the time the epitome of advanced interceptors – would be reassessed, re-designed and refined for the demands of the global war and demanding air campaigns that lay ahead. Nor that the direct successors of these designs would be pitted against each other in air combat in less than five years.

Tempest V NV969/SA-A of Sqn Ldr Warren E. Schrader RNZAF, CO of No. 486 Sqn, at Hustedt in April 1945. Schrader was the second highest-scoring pilot on Tempests, claiming 11 and 2 shared aircraft shot down with the Hawker fighter. Five of his victims were Fw 190s, and four of them fell to NV969. On 1 May Schrader was promoted to the rank of wing commander and posted to take over No. 616 Sqn, flying Meteor IIIs. (CT Collection)

CHRONOLOGY

1893
5 August — Sydney Camm, Hawker's Chief Designer, born in Windsor, England

1898
24 February — Kurt Tank, designer of the Fw 190D-9, born in Bromberg-Schwedenhöhe, Prussia.

1924
1 January — Focke-Wulf Flugzeugbau AG established in Bremen (renamed from Bremer Flugzeugbau AG, formed 23 October 1923).

1933
18 May — Hawker Aircraft Limited established at Kingston upon Thames from H. G. Hawker Engineering Company.

1937
September — *Reichsluftfahrtministerium* (RLM) issues specification to Focke-Wulf for a fighter with performance superior to that of the Messerschmitt Bf 109.

1939
1 June — Fw 190 V1 makes maiden flight in Bremen with Focke-Wulf Chief Test Pilot Flugkapitän Hans Sander at the controls.

1940
March — Hawker produce several design studies aimed at improving the Typhoon, especially its thick wing section.

1941
July — RLM asks Messerschmitt and Focke-Wulf for designs for a high-altitude interceptor and reconnaissance aircraft.

November — Two prototypes of Typhoon II ordered – renamed 'Tempest'.

November — An inverted V12 Junkers Jumo 213A engine is installed into an Fw 190 airframe as an alternative to the BMW 801C-1.

1942
June — Proposed Tempest V prototype to be fitted with Sabre II engine, maximum power 2,180hp.

2 September — Maiden flight of Tempest V prototype HM595 with Hawker Chief Experimental Test Pilot Phillip Lucas at the controls.

26 September — Maiden flight of Jumo-powered Fw 190D-9 prototype V17 flown by Sander. This aircraft does not have the fuselage extension seen on later models.

1943
1 June — Formation of RAF's Tactical Air Force.

21 June — First production Tempest V JN729 flies, flown by Bill Humble.

23 November — Tactical Air Force renamed 2nd Tactical Air Force.

1944
12 June — Maiden flight of first 'true' D-9 prototype, V53, converted from an Fw 190A-8 with engine capable of being fitted with cannon.

20 September — First four Fw 190D-9s delivered to III./JG 54 at Oldenburg, in northern Germany.

Beginning – JN729, the first production Tempest V built at Langley of an initial run of 100 machines, banks over for the camera during a test flight. Hawker used the aircraft for trials. (The Aviation Historian)

28 September	First Tempest Vs of Nos. 3, 56 and 486 Sqns join No. 122 Wing at B60 Grimbergen.
28 September	Hauptmann Robert Weiss of III./JG 54 claims first victory in a Fw 190D-9 (a photo-reconnaissance unit Spitfire PR XI of No. 541 Sqn).
29 September	First combat activity involving Tempest Vs against ('short-nose') Fw 190s takes place within 24 hours of arrival. Pilots of No. 56 Sqn claim Tempest's first victories against Fw 190s in northwestern Europe.
27 December	First action between Tempest Vs and Fw 190D-9s fought over Paderborn. No. 486 Sqn and III./JG 54 are the two units involved.

DESIGN AND DEVELOPMENT

TEMPEST V

The development of the Tempest, the last of Sydney Camm's designs to see operational service during World War II, lay in what can best be described metaphorically, but also with truth, as 'winds of change'. As early as 1936, at the Hawker design office in Kingston, Camm had begun to look towards a new, single-seat interceptor design capable of 400mph that would supersede the Hurricane. His search commenced only months after the flight of the Hurricane prototype on 6 November 1935 and around a year before the first production aircraft flew at Brooklands on 12 October 1937. Once the Hurricane was in full-scale production in late 1939, his intentions focused more closely on his longer-term goal.

Under the specification 'F.18/37', and despite concern on the part of the Air Ministry, which expressed reservations about the installation of more powerful engines in single-seat fighter airframes, Camm drew up two variations of the same design, one powered by a 1,760hp Rolls-Royce Vulture engine, the other by the 2,180hp Napier Sabre.

While the Sabre was hampered by development problems, the Vulture won the day in terms of availability for what had been christened the 'Tornado', and in December 1938 Rolls-Royce delivered an example for fitting into the Tornado prototype then under construction. Seven months later, this first aircraft was transferred from Kingston to Langley, in Berkshire, and the maiden flight was made from there on

6 October 1939. An impressive maximum speed of more than 380mph was attained, and following further flight tests, the Air Ministry placed an order for 500 new Tornado fighters.

However, this positive turn of events faded when problems began to occur with the Vulture's connecting rods, which were prone to failure – Vulture-powered Avro Manchester twin-engined bombers suffered particularly badly from this issue. It had also been to A. V. Roe & Co, manufacturers of the ill-fated Manchester, that production of the Tornado had been assigned, but output of the bomber fell away when issues with the Vulture began to materialise and a number of them were lost as a direct result. Consequently, Rolls-Royce terminated production of the Vulture so as to concentrate on the Merlin. Amidst all this, just one production Tornado had emerged, which was ultimately transferred to Rotol Ltd at Staverton, in Gloucestershire, and de Havilland Propellers at Hatfield, in Hertfordshire, for the testing of propellers.

In early 1940, Hawker relocated its design office to nearby Esher, in Surrey – a timely move given that later that year a Luftwaffe bomb fell on the company's Production Process Department housed in a building just across the road from the old design office in Kingston. It was around the time of the move from Kingston to Esher that Camm proposed the 2,210hp 18-cylinder Bristol Centaurus radial engine as a replacement for the troublesome Vulture. Although tests on a second prototype Tornado powered by the Bristol engine achieved a maximum speed of 402mph, it was too late and the Tornado project was cancelled.

Undaunted, Camm and his team turned to the Napier Sabre version, which was given the name 'Typhoon'. The prototype flew in February 1940, with flight-testing continuing until September 1941 when the first production aircraft built by Gloster were delivered, culminating in 150 Typhoons by the end of the year. Again, problems – some resulting in write-offs – dogged the type. These centred around the unreliability of the engine and, an aspect that was not evident until mid-1942, the structural failure of the rear fuselage in front of the tailplane. It took a year to pin this down to elevator

The first Tempest prototype to fly as a Mk V was HM595. It is seen here at Langley in September 1942 in its initial form, the aircraft incorporating a Typhoon-style canopy, fin and rudder. (CT Collection)

flutter caused by failure of the mass balance mounting. No fewer than 16 aircraft were lost, and only one pilot survived, before modifications greatly reduced the failure rate – but never completely cured it. Amongst those killed was Hawker test pilot Kenneth Seth-Smith, who perished when the elevator balance weight bracket of his Typhoon cracked as a result of fatigue.

Despite these initial challenges, it was recognized that the Typhoon *did* possess superlative low-level capabilities, and so trials commenced with various rocket, bomb and cannon weapons configurations intended for ground attack work. In this, the Typhoon excelled, and thus the decision was taken henceforward to switch the aircraft from the interceptor role to that of dedicated fighter-bomber – a task fulfilled up to that point by ground attack sub-variants of the Hurricane II.

It was during this process of change that the Air Ministry issued Hawker with yet another interceptor specification, namely F.10/41. Dialogue between the Ministry's Director of Technical Development and Sydney Camm resulted in the notion that a thinner wing could be incorporated into the existing Typhoon together with wing leading edge radiators, similar to those used by de Havilland Mosquito, and a new version of the Sabre engine which, it was believed, would offer increased performance.

Following analysis and assessment, Camm's project team concluded that speeds of considerably more than 400mph could be attained in level flight, with 500mph or more being achievable in a dive. Comparatively, at high speeds, the thick wings of the Hurricane and the Typhoon had a US NACA (National Advisory Committee for Aeronautics) four-digit series wing section with a thickness to chord ratio of 19.5 per cent (root) to 12 per cent tip. While this provided strength and adequate room for fuel and armament, it also caused buffeting and loss of aileron control, as well as a marked increase in drag as speeds approached 500mph. This in turn adversely affected the use of the gunsight for accurate targeting when engaging an opponent in aerial combat.

Despite some initial reluctance to accept that a thinner wing could be as strong as a thicker section when designed well, Camm agreed to conduct high-speed tests with a Typhoon. His view had possibly been influenced by investigations conducted in March 1940 into the new, low-drag laminar flow wing developed by NACA that had been incorporated into the North American P-51 Mustang. Furthermore, following subsequent debriefing with Hawker test pilots, Camm came to accept that a thinner wing was what was needed to create a high-speed interceptor version of his fighter-bomber. This project, known as Hawker P.1012, was soon christened Typhoon II, and it would pave the way for what would become the Tempest.

Camm's project team set to work designing the new wing in detail, and proffered its plans to the Air Ministry officially as F.10/41. The design of the wing had a maximum thickness to chord ratio of 14.5 per cent at the root, tapering to ten per cent at the tip. The maximum point of

The 2,180hp, 24-cylinder, water-cooled Napier Sabre II engine as installed in the Tempest V. It was technologically advanced and powerful, but complex. Note the good all-round vision offered by the bubble canopy and the armoured headrest fitted above the pilot's seat. (CT Collection)

thickness in the wing of the Tempest was set back at 37.5 per cent of the chord, as against 30 per cent for the wing of the Typhoon. The new wing meant that fuel accommodation had to be reviewed, and the solution was found by moving the engine forward 21 inches and placing a 76-gallon tank between the firewall and the oil tank.

The Air Ministry needed little convincing as to the merit of Camm's latest fighter design, and in August 1942 an initial order of 400 aircraft was placed, despite the flight of a prototype Tempest not occurring until 2 September that same year. However, because of problems with the Napier Sabre IV engine installed into the first prototype, this sleek-looking machine – Mk I HM599, fitted uniquely with wing leading edge radiators intended to reduce drag – did not take to the air until February 1943. When it did though, it climbed to 24,500ft and comfortably reached 466mph in level flight. Nevertheless, the issues with the Sabre IV never went away and Napier cancelled further work on it, leaving HM599 as the only airframe with the wing radiators.

The remaining five Tempest prototypes emerged as the Mk II, of which two examples, LA602 and LA607 (the fastest of the batch as it transpired), were built, fitted with the 2,520hp Centaurus IV air-cooled radial engine. They were followed by Mk III LA610, built with a Rolls-Royce Griffon IIB engine, Mk IV LA614, re-engined initially with a Griffon IIB, which was replaced by the Griffon 61 power egg, and Mk V HM595, fitted with a 2,180hp Sabre II.

Designed by Maj Frank Halford, the Sabre was the third in a series of engines commencing with the Rapier and the Dagger that were produced by the firm of D. Napier & Son. With 24 water-cooled cylinders and single sleeve valves, and at 36.7 litres running at 3,700rpm, the Sabre was the largest of the three and would ultimately develop 3,100hp. Early examples had been hand-built and fitted by skilled engineers and mechanics at the Napier factory in west London and at a shadow factory in Liverpool. The engine had first been tested in 1939 in a Fairey Battle, but later production examples lacked this refinement. The mechanics suffered as a result, especially when placed under the rigours of operational service.

The main issue was traced to the sleeves and their drives, the former being made

The Tempest I prototype in flight, fitted with a later style one-piece canopy. The Tempest I was the fastest of the type, but delays affecting the Napier Sabre IV meant development stalled. (CT Collection)

TEMPEST V

33ft 8in.

16ft 1in.

41ft 0in.

from nitrided chrome molybdenum steel alloy forging that were prone to seizure and loss of compression. This problem was eventually solved by employing nitrided austenitic forgings applied with tooling made by the Bristol Aeroplane Company. On 23 November 1942 Napier & Son was taken over by English Electric. Even with revised design, the engine proved a tricky beast – technologically advanced and powerful, but complex. Furthermore, there were problems associated with poor workmanship in the form of inadequately cleaned castings, broken piston rings and cuttings left inside supposedly 'finished' engines.

Despite these problems, from 1941 through to 1945 successive Sabre variants with four-barrel SU carburettors, Hobson-RAE single-point injection carburettors and two- and single-sided blower impellers were installed in the progressive Tempest variants. However, because of the delays affecting the Sabre IV and Centaurus engines, and the re-design required for the Griffon, the Tempest V became ready to fly before the others. HM595 flew for the first time on 2 September 1942 with Hawker Chief Experimental Test Pilot Phillip G. Lucas at the controls. The aircraft had the appearance of a hybrid, with the framed canopy of the Typhoon, but with an extended nose and a vertical tail surface that was larger as a result of a new fin fillet and a horizontal tail expanded by a greater span and chord. The new wing was also found to have improved handling at speed.

The question of wing armament was a vexed one, however. One option was for three 20mm cannon in each wing, another was for two 20mm weapons, or a single cannon with either a 0.5-in. machine gun or a pair of 0.303-in. machine guns. However, the new 'thin' wing precluded these proposals, and eventually the RAF settled on two 20mm Hispano Mk II cannon (with 200 rounds per gun) per wing.

On 24 February 1943, the Tempest I finally took to the skies, generally performing well, with only some minor areas of concern such as elevator control at lower speeds and a sluggish throttle. The Mk I would eventually achieve a top speed of 466mph at 24,500ft.

That same month, three RAF test pilots from the Aeroplane and Armament Experimental Establishment (A&AEE) flew Mk V HM595, which they noted was pleasant to fly and handled well. Although the Mk V prototype had a built-up cockpit canopy with a car-type entry door of the type found in early Typhoons, the pilots were

OPPOSITE

Tempest V EJ719/JF-R of No. 3 Sqn is seen as it would have appeared in December 1944 at B.80 Volkel after months of regular service in Britain with the ADGB flying V1 interception operations followed by punishing missions with 2nd TAF in northwest Europe. The aircraft is finished in the standard disruptive pattern of Dark Green over Ocean Grey, with the underside in Medium Sea Grey. The spinner was in black and the aircraft carried the reduced form 18-inch-wide black and white identification stripes on the underside of the fuselage. The fighter is carrying underwing 45-gallon drop tanks. EJ719 met its end when it was shot down by flak near Dulmen on 1 January 1945, as a result of which its pilot, V1 ace Flg Off Ron Pottinger, bailed out and was captured.

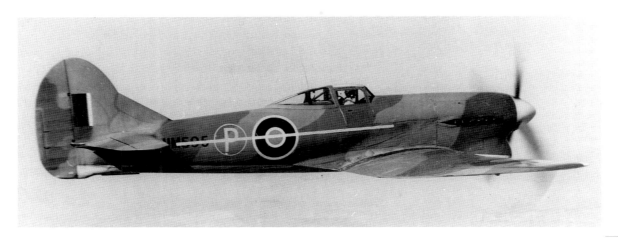

HM595 is seen here whilst undergoing testing at the A&AEE after being fitted with a larger tailplane and interim fin extension for handling trials. (CT Collection)

An extra 21-inch bay was incorporated into the Tempest fuselage between the firewall and the oil tank to accommodate a 76-gallon fuel tank. (CT Collection)

also encouraged by the new sliding hood intended for the Tempest, which they were able to examine fitted to a Typhoon.

It was the lingering delays associated with the Napier Sabre IV and the lack of confidence shown by the Air Ministry in the wing radiators, however, that sealed the fate of the Tempest I and led to faith being placed in the Mk V. An order for a production run of 100 examples of the latter aircraft was placed with Hawker, and these would be built in the company's factory at Langley from June 1943. Eventually, some 1,400 Tempests would be manufactured here. Further development of the Griffon-engined Mks III and IV was also terminated (with the Rolls-Royce powerplant generally being seen as the engine for the Spitfire), while work on the Centaurus-powered Mk II continued.

On 21 June 1943, the first production Series I Tempest V, JN729, took to the air flown by Hawker test pilot Bill Humble, who had taken an active role in the type's development. All went well. Series I aircraft were converted Typhoons, distinguishable by the extended barrels of their 20mm Mk II Hispano cannon that protruded nearly eight inches ahead of the wing leading edge, unlike all subsequent series which had shorter-barrelled cannon. There was great benefit in the original design for the guns to be mounted outside the propeller disc and almost entirely encapsulated within the wing, thus minimising drag. Access to the aileron cable runs was gained via the ammunition bay panels, while the location of the cannon breaches behind the rear wing spar allowed easy access, servicing and removal, the guns being simply pulled out from the rear.

In the autumn, the third production machine, JN731, underwent tests at the A&AEE Boscombe Down, in Wiltshire. The aircraft flew at 432mph at 18,400ft, while down at 6,600ft it managed 411mph. At sea level, speed was 376mph. Again, the reaction to performance, handling and response was generally satisfactory, with the view from the cockpit considered excellent, although there was some criticism of the heavy ailerons and poor rate of roll – aspects which would be cured by the incorporation of spring-tab ailerons. The aircraft could also develop a pronounced swing on take-off unless the throttle was opened very smoothly and rudder corrections quickly applied. Finally, landing the five-ton Tempest at 100mph was no easy task, especially with the attendant risk of a burst tyre and ensuing high-speed ground-loop.

As British aviation historians Chris Thomas and Christopher Shores have succinctly noted, 'It was apparent that with a little more refinement the RAF was about to receive its most potent medium- and low-level fighter yet.' Indeed, the development of the Tempest was timely, for in Germany, a new, formidable fighter had appeared that threatened to have a significant impact on contemporary British types.

Fw 190D-9

Arguably, the Focke-Wulf Fw 190 evolved into wartime Germany's most effective fighter, offering the Luftwaffe the benefit of manoeuvrability combined with stability as a formidable gun platform and the flexibility to perform as an air superiority fighter, a heavily armed and armoured interceptor and as an ordnance-carrying ground attack aircraft. However, this superlative machine had its Achilles' heel, for when the first Fw 190A-2s entered operational service with *Stab*/JG 26 and I./JG 26 on the Channel Front in July 1941, it became apparent quite quickly that the type's performance at high-altitude was weak.

The Fw 190A-2 was powered by the 1,500hp BMW 801C-1 and 1,600 hp C-2 radial engines. From the start, and during initial testing in 1940 and early 1941, this engine was plagued with faults. Crews and technicians of the Luftwaffe's dedicated test unit *Erprobungsstaffel* 190 at Rechlin, therefore, were forced to undertake considerable trouble-shooting. Finally, by August 1941, the engine was deemed safe enough to allow the first Fw 190A-1 production machines to be handed over to 6./JG 26, which at the time was based in Belgium. Unfortunately, the problems persisted, with nine Fw 190s crashing in August–September 1941. The finger of blame was pointed at BMW, whose engines continued to be plagued by overheating and compressor damage.

There were also delays in deliveries associated with failings afflicting the anticipated 1,700hp BMW 801D. This engine, fitted in the Fw 190A-3 (in production from late 1941), benefited from uprated power achieved by increasing the compression ratio in the cylinders and refinements to the two-speed supercharger. Nevertheless, it was found to suffer from a fall in performance above 19,750ft.

A wooden wind tunnel model of the planned Fw 190D-1 showing the earliest 'Langnase' design. Despite the spinner hole, it was not foreseen that this variant was to have an engine cannon. The D-1 and the following D-2 were abandoned at an early stage in any case and were replaced by the D-9. (EN-Archive)

Despite this worrying scenario, since early 1941 Kurt Tank had been working on a re-design of the Fw 190 that would incorporate a different powerplant capable of functioning effectively at altitudes higher than those then achievable. In his post-war memoirs, Tank summarises succinctly the prevailing situation at the time:

Hardly was the Fw 190 flying at the beginning of the war before it had to be extensively redesigned, enlarged and made more powerful still. In no time at all, the requirements of very many pieces of auxiliary equipment connected with the armament and communications of the plane forced up its weight, and at the same time new and more powerful engines were becoming available.

In November 1941, under the project designation 'Ra-8', Focke-Wulf decided to install a Junkers Jumo 213A inverted V12 engine into the airframe of an Fw 190, while tests also proceeded with a Daimler-Benz DB 603 inline inverted V12 – this option was ultimately dropped in favour of the Jumo unit. The Jumo 213's edge came in the form of a pressurised cooling system and, with high boost settings, was designed to produce 1,750hp at 3,250rpm. In a clever move, the Junkers design team placed the mounting points in exactly the same locations as those for the DB 603. Although this meant easy interchange, the supercharger intake was to be found on the left side of the DB 603, while in the case of the Jumo it was on the right. The Jumo 213 also had a strengthened crankshaft and engine block, with smaller external dimensions than the Daimler-Benz motor, although it did retain the same bore and stroke.

The first aircraft to be fitted with a Jumo 213A was Wk-Nr. 0039 CF+OX, which was prototype V17. This Fw 190, with its *'Langnase'* ('long nose') as a result of the engine installation, also featured a tail unit that was similar in shape to what would appear in the later Ta 152 high-altitude interceptor. It took to the air for the first time on 26 September 1942 from Hannover-Langenhagen, flown by Focke-Wulf chief test pilot Flugkapitän Hans Sander. There were some initial teething problems with the installation, and after Kurt Melhorn had made the eighth test flight in V17 on

The freshly finished 20th prototype D-9 V20 TH+IG was originally intended as a test-bed for the DB 603. It was fitted with a Jumo 213A-1 engine, however, and made its inaugural flight on 23 November 1943 with Hans Sander at the controls. Unarmed, the prototype was used to demonstrate Tank's design to RLM personnel. (EN-Archive)

4 December 1942, he reported that 'the engine is still running very roughly so that proper testing cannot be carried out.' In January 1943 the aircraft was returned to the workshops for fitting with a pre-production Jumo 213A-0.

Focke-Wulf persisted with the trials throughout 1943, Sander completing three test flights in V17 on 27 February, for example. The aircraft had its radio equipment removed and replaced by a ballast load of 290lb, with 26lb in the tail fin and 33lb in the jacking tube. Unfortunately, extreme vibration made the machine impossible to fly, casting heavy doubts over any chance of it becoming a combat-ready fighter since, primarily, such vibration would greatly hamper use of a reflector gunsight. More flights were undertaken in March by Sander, his fellow test-pilot Bernhard Märschel and Hauptmann Otto Behrens, a Luftwaffe fighter technician from Rechlin. Still the Jumo was viewed as unfavourable compared to the earlier BMW engine, despite the fitting of new bearings. Beside long-running coolant leaks, oil was now found to be routinely seeping onto the floor of the cockpit when the aircraft was aloft.

On 30 April V17 was transferred to Rechlin for further assessment in the hope of solving these problems. It was discovered that the vibration was caused by crankshaft resonance in the continuous speed range, and a solution was soon found in the form of a spoke wheel inserted between the crankshaft and the propeller. This duly shifted the resonance into an rpm range that was not disruptive. A change in the cylinder firing sequence reduced vibration levels even further, although this in turn reduced the engine's performance by a full eight per cent because the exhaust and intake lines had been optimised for the original firing sequence. Nevertheless, by June 1943, the 185 engines thus far completed at Junkers' Dessau plant had been modified accordingly.

During the summer V17 returned from Rechlin to Focke-Wulf, where it was fitted with a Jumo 213A-1 and a streamlined cowling but still lacked armament.

The technical issues surrounding the Jumo powerplant persisted for more than a year, prompting General-Ingenieur Wolfram Eisenlohr, head of the engine department in the RLM, to lament:

> The neglect under which matters of engine development have long suffered have now led to a critical lack of developmental capacity. A glance at other countries shows that research into powerplant matters abroad have been handled much more favourably than here.

In May 1944 V17 was refitted with a Jumo 213A-2 that drove a wooden VS 9 propeller. The Junkers engine was some 24 inches longer than the BMW 801, which meant the aircraft had to be modified at the Focke-Wulf plant at Adelheide in late April. Its fuselage was extended by 20 inches just ahead of the tail assembly to offset this. In this configuration, the machine became V17/U1 – the first true Fw 190D-9 prototype. Testing went reasonably well, with Märschel completing the inaugural flight on 17 May when he flew it back to Hannover-Langenhagen. Here, it underwent extensive trials, with test pilots generally reporting that the Jumo 213A offered a great improvement at altitude over the BMW 801D. Furthermore, thanks to the D-9's reduced drag as a result of its a narrower radiator profile, it was faster than the radial-engined Fw 190 in a dive.

In a further stage of development, in June–July 1944, because of 'difficulties with existing prototypes', the airframes of two early Fw 190A-8s were reconfigured under the suffix D-9 ('D' being given the moniker *Dora*) – a designation that seems to have first been used in a Focke-Wulf drawing dating from January 1944. These aircraft were to be made available 'immediately' at Adelheide under the prototype numbers V53 and V54. The Fw 190A-8 variant was by far the most numerous and most potent Focke-Wulf heavy fighter to be built, and it became the Luftwaffe's main close-range interceptor for operations against USAAF heavy bombers throughout 1944–45.

The January 1944 drawing incorporated an extended fuselage and tail assembly, along with strengthening of the forward fuselage and wing centre section and provision for a Jumo 213A engine.

The first to be converted was Wk-Nr. 170003, the third A-8 to be built, which became V53 (coded DU+JC) in the D-9 programme. However, this prototype was fitted with a Jumo 213C at the Focke-Wulf plant at Sorau, in Silesia. Essentially an A-model Jumo engine with rearranged secondary equipment (such as supercharger and oil pump), it was capable of, and designed from the outset for, the fitment of a centreline cannon firing through an opening for a blast tube in the propeller hub. This had the advantage of a gun being more along a pilot's line of sight, as well as offering less impact on speed and manoeuvrability. A disadvantage, however, was the recoil associated with a centrally-mounted weapon and the impact it had on the engine, leading to potential mechanical problems and possible damage.

When the aircraft made its first flight on 12 June 1944, it retained the original A-8 wing armament comprising four 20mm MG 151/20E cannon and a pair of 13mm MG 131 machine guns mounted over the engine. Testing of V53 was rigorous, with no fewer than 100 flights being made before it was eventually reassigned as an armaments test aircraft for the new Ta 152B-5, at which point it became V68.

Fw 190A-8 Wk-Nr. 174024, coded BH+RX, was an aircraft that had suffered some damage on 29 May. Reconfigured as D-9 V54, its maiden flight took place on 26 July 1944 and its last on 4 August at Focke-Wulf's Langenhagen plant when it was flown by Flugkapitän Sander. The main task of V54 was to trial the MW 50 methanol-water power-boosting system, for which a 115-litre tank was installed. There is some documentary evidence to suggest that the original plan was for V54 to test the GM-1 nitrous oxide-based injection power-boosting system developed by Otto Lutz in 1940.

MW 50 was a solution of 50 per cent methanol, 49.5 per cent water and 0.5 per cent anti-corrosive fluid, the liquid being injected directly into the supercharger for limited periods not exceeding ten minutes. In air combat, the boost increased the power of a Jumo 213 engine by at least 300hp to 2,000hp for short periods. Such a system came with the added benefit of needing only the installation of purpose-made spark plugs to modify the engine. However, its one side-effect was that the corrosive nature of methanol reduced engine life.

Production of the Fw 190D-9 was planned to commence in August, but on the 5th there was a setback when both the A-8 conversions were damaged as a result of an American bombing raid on Langenhagen. V53 escaped with light damage rated at five per cent, but V54 suffered 80 per cent damage and was written off. Nevertheless, series production did start at Focke-Wulf's Cottbus and Sorau plants later in the

Fw 190D-9

33ft 5.5in.

11ft 0in.

34ft 5in.

The Jumo 213A as installed in the prototype D-9 V53 at Focke-Wulf's Sorau plant, with its strong engine mount. The curved tank, another of which was fitted to the other side of the unit, was an auxiliary coolant tank. By the time production-standard Jumo 213 engines reached the aircraft assembly lines, they were three years behind schedule. (EN-Archive)

month, as well as at the Gerhard Fieseler Werke at Kassel-Waldau and at the Ago Oschersleben and Arbeitsgemeinschaft Roland plants. The first production machines rolled out of the assembly halls at Sorau towards the end of August, with Sander taking Wk-Nr. 210001 TR+SA up on the 31st, while Hauptmann Schmitz flew the second example, Wk-Nr. 210002 TR+SB, on 15 September. Both aircraft did suffer from minor teething problems, but series production was now underway.

Having been repaired after the August attack on Langenhagen, V53 had had its outboard wing MG 151s removed and the two inboard weapons replaced by 30mm MK 103 cannon by late 1944. In such a configuration the aircraft was redesignated V68. V17 was still available for testing, despite its 'official' testing life having ended on 6 July at the *Erprobungsstelle* at Rechlin. Wk-Nr. 210001 was fitted with two MG 131 machine guns above the engine and two MG 151 cannon in the wing roots. Problems were still being experienced with the Jumo 213A-1, however. The second machine to be turned out, Wk-Nr. 210002, had the same armament and took to the air on 15 September flown by Hauptmann Schmitz. It was found during subsequent tests in this aircraft that 'while climbing at combat power, with all flaps set to flush at 9,000m [29,500ft], an increase of over 2m [6.5ft]/sec in the rate of climb, as well as an increase of the service ceiling to 10,500m [34,500ft], could be obtained.'

In one test to measure engine temperature during a climb in Wk-Nr. 210001 at Langenhagen on 20 October, it was noted that:

The radiator coolant inlet and outlet temperatures, as well as the lubricant and supercharger air temperatures at the engine entrance, were taken using combat power climb with 20 degrees angle radiator flap opening. Since the last flight had to be broken off because of weather and engine breakdown, the height of peak temperature was just reached at 6000m [19,685ft] altitude.

Teething problems persisted, however, as illustrated by a report prepared at Langenhagen on 24 October:

As delivered, substantial gaps were present in the engine, in particular in the connection from the cowl to the wing. In order to check for their influence on level speeds, performance comparison flights were carried out in the low supercharger range, before and after sealing of all existing gaps. After conclusion of the trials in the initial condition, an even gap width at the transition from the cowl to the wing had to be ensured, first by shifting of the lower engine cover against the propeller direction of rotation, since substantial differences arose by the engine torque in flight. Then the sealing of the fairing was made by means of rubber gaskets and metal strips.

Nevertheless, as production stepped up at Cottbus and Sorau, plans were made to manufacture four D-9s per day, but such a scale of output would not be reached until November, when, in addition to the Focke-Wulf, Fieseler and Roland plants (Ago was eventually dropped from the programme), Mimetall at Erfurt-Nord was added. The first Fw 190D-9 to be delivered to an operational Luftwaffe unit was Wk-Nr. 210003.

Fw 190D-9 Wk-Nr. 211934 of II./JG 6, assigned to that *Gruppe*'s Technical Officer, seen at Fürth after surrendering to American forces. Note the supercharger intake on the right side of the cowling and the Junkers VS 9 wooden constant-speed hydraulic variable-pitch propeller with its broad chord blades. Also visible beneath the fuselage are the DF loop at rear and antennae for the FuG 25a IFF and FuG 16ZY VHF transceivers. (EN-Archive)

TECHNICAL
SPECIFICATIONS

Tempest V

As an aircraft, in terms of structure, the Tempest V owed much to the Hurricane and the Typhoon, but with some innovative features of its own. The Tempest's skin was flush-riveted, but in places where it was of light gauge, the rivetting process caused some minor dishing of the metal, resulting in the rivet lines being visible. The wing offered an improvement over the Typhoon because of the superior, flush-riveted surface finish that was essential on a high-performance laminar flow air foil. In the Typhoon II (the Tempest I), the wingspan was 43ft (and thus greater than that of the Typhoon at 41 ft), although it is not believed this variant ever flew. The wing area was also greater at 302 sq ft over 278 sq ft. At the rear fuselage, the panels were lap-pointed, not butt-jointed, with the higher plates overlapping the lower ones.

An initial run of some 50 aircraft were built using rear fuselages from a cancelled Typhoon contract. These took the form of a monocoque rear section, while the centre section contained the cockpit and the front section held the engine, with bearers fitted to carry the Sabre II. The tail and fin assembly were of stressed skin construction and the control surfaces covered in metal, except the rudder which was fabric-covered. The wing was of a two-spar design with ribs, with the light alloy skin stiffened by span-wise stringers. The flat centre section minimised the length of the undercarriage legs, and there were outer panels with 5.5 degrees of dihedral.

Standard wingspan settled at 41ft, and an additional 30-gallon tank was built into the leading edge of the port wing root, giving later Tempest Vs a total internal fuel capacity of 162 gallons. The Tempest was also fitted with two specially designed, streamlined, drop tanks of 90 gallons capacity. Range without the drop tanks was given as 740 miles, but with them, 1,530 miles.

The Tempest also featured a redesigned undercarriage to the Typhoon, with longer oleo legs and a wider track of 16ft which improved stability when landing at speeds of around 110mph, as well as allowing sufficient clearance for the 14ft-diameter de Havilland four-blade propeller. Early Tempests used five-spoke Typhoon wheels fitted with slimmer tyres. These were soon changed to a slimmer, four-spoke design with specially made tyres because of the thin wing/wheel-bay space. The tailwheel was retractable and fully enclosed by small doors, and could be fitted with a plain tyre made by Dunlop or a Dunlop-Marstrand 'twin-contact' anti-shimmy tyre. The tailwheel retracted forwards hydraulically into the fuselage, and once retracted it was fully enclosed by two doors.

Externally, the noticeable difference between a Series I aircraft and the following Series II was that the Hispano 20mm Mk II cannon of the former variant protruded eight inches ahead of the wing leading edge. This weapon was a license-built version of the French Hispano-Suiza HS.404 that had first been used as a fighter gun in the Westland Whirlwind in 1940. British engineers went on to develop a belt-feeding mechanism that was used by both the RAF and the Fleet Air Arm in 1941 in a slightly

The Tempest V could take punishment – No. 222 Sqn's SN165/ZD-V, seen here at B.91 Kluis in April 1945, was hit by flak as it carried out an attack on Fassberg airfield. While making a strafing run, the cockpit was hit and the pilot's head armour broke off, rendering Sqn Ldr E. B. Lyons semi-conscious. He nevertheless managed to return to base. Note also the damage to the leading edge of the horizontal stabiliser. (CT Collection)

25

TEMPEST V ARMAMENT

Wing armament for the Tempest V evolved from the first 100 aircraft being fitted with two 20mm Hispano Mk II cannon (200 rounds per gun) mounted in each wing centre section and known as Series 1 aircraft, to the subsequent production run carrying shorter-barrelled Hispano Mk V guns, known as Series 2 types. In the Series 1, the barrels projected some eight inches in front of the wing leading edge, while in Series 2 aircraft (as depicted here) there was virtually no projection, with the inner guns being completely contained within the wing and the muzzle of the outer weapons just sitting proud of the leading edge.

modified form as the Hispano Mk II. This weapon replaced the eight Browning 0.303-in. machine guns in the Hurricane IIC and in the Spitfire VC, and would go on to be installed in later mark Spitfires, as well as the Typhoon and Tempest. The Hispano Mk II fired a 4.58oz 20mm x 110mm projectile with a muzzle velocity of between 2,750–2,900ft per second, depending on barrel length. The rate of fire was between 600 and 850 rounds per minute. It was 7ft 9in long and weighed between 93–110lbs. In the Tempest V, the cannon were armed with 200 rounds per gun, and the wings' elliptical shape gave a deeper chord to accommodate the cannon and their ammunition. Internally, the gunsight was of the standard reflector type.

The tail unit was reinforced by being fixed to the rear of the fuselage by means of riveted fish plates. Because Series I machines were adapted Typhoon airframes, the rear spar fitting was cranked in order to pick up the fuselage lugs, which, in the Typhoon, were too high to facilitate direct attachment. As a result, the top wing root fillet fairing incorporated a bulge in it to clear this fitting.

During initial assessment with the third production Mk V JN731 at the A&AEE at Boscombe Down, the view from the cockpit was considered to be excellent. On 8 January 1944, this aircraft was dispatched to the Air Fighting Development Unit (AFDU) at Wittering, in Cambridgeshire, where it underwent comparison trials

against contemporary Allied aircraft, as well as captured German fighters. The AFDU tests revealed a mixed bag of positives and negatives. As with the service test pilots at the A&AEE, the assessors at Wittering found the Tempest to have superb all-round vision while taking off, landing, in formation and when dogfighting, bettering any Allied fighter in service.

When pitted against its Typhoon stablemate (albeit one fitted with the old, framed-style canopy), the Tempest proved itself to be 15–20mph faster at maximum speed at various altitudes, and its rate of climb was about 300ft per minute better at maximum rate, while it was also superior in both 'zoom' climb and in the dive. This greater speed margin was offset by a lower fuel tankage of 132 gallons (as a result of the elliptical wing design losing the leading edge fuel tanks found in the Typhoon) compared to the Typhoon's 154 gallons. However, the Sabre IIB engine ran smoothly, while the control surfaces all demonstrated an improvement over the Typhoon. The loss of fuel space would be rectified by the incorporation of a new 21-inch bay in front of the cockpit holding a 76-gallon tank. Additionally, two inter-spar wing tanks, each of 28 gallons, were fitted on either side of the centre-section.

In tests against the Mustang III, Spitfire XIV, Bf 109G and Fw 190A (the latter two were captured examples), the Tempest was faster than all of them below 20,000ft – by between 15–20mph against the Allied types and 40–50mph against the German aircraft. The Mustang and Spitfire outpaced the Tempest at higher altitudes, and while the Bf 109G was an equal to the Tempest, the British fighter took the lead over the Focke-Wulf. In terms of manoeuvrability, both the Mustang and the Spitfire had the edge over the Tempest in the turn, although the latter could turn tighter than the Bf 109 and was equal to the Fw 190. In roll rate, the Tempest did not measure up to the Mustang, Spitfire or Fw 190, although at speeds in excess of 350mph, it proved the winner over the Spitfire. Against the Bf 109, it was roughly the same when below 350mph, but above it, the Tempest could outstrip the Messerschmitt by making a quick change of bank and direction. The AFDU concluded that the Tempest V out-performed the Typhoon emphatically, and up to medium altitude was faster than any other fighter.

Having removed the gun access panel, an armourer of No. 41 Sqn carefully feeds a belt of 20mm ammunition into the left wing magazine for a Tempest V's Hispano cannon at B.156 Lübeck in the winter of 1945–46. The cylindrical feed unit of the gun is also visible. (CT Collection)

After the first 100 aircraft, the remaining 701 Tempest Vs were built to Series II specification. Armament in Series II Tempest Vs came in the form of the Hispano Mk V, the barrel of which was shorter than the Mk II and virtually enclosed within the wing. This weapon was lighter and had a higher rate of fire than its predecessor, although at the expense of some muzzle velocity. The shorter barrels and smaller feed motors resulted in more compact installation within the wings of the Tempest V.

Generally, Series II aircraft also benefited from cheaper components that required fewer man hours to make and were of a lighter weight. For example, the tubular steel fuselage rear spar pick-up was replaced by a one-piece casting that gave a direct pick-up, making a much simpler structural joint. The rear fuselage was not reinforced and, unlike Series I machines, had a detachable tail unit.

In assessing the Tempest V, Wg Cdr Roland Beamont viewed it as being the direct successor to the Typhoon, but with most of the shortcomings of that aircraft eliminated or improved. 'Each flight,' he said, 'brought greater enjoyment of, and confidence in, the crisp ailerons, firm though responsive elevator and good directional stability and damping, giving high promise of superior gun-aiming capability, exhilarating performance and, with all this, magnificent combat vision.'

Armourers spool a belt of 20mm shells into the feed mechanism of a No. 41 Sqn Tempest V's Hispano wing cannon. The unit replaced its Spitfire XIVs with Tempest Vs in September 1945 while based at B.156 Lübeck. (CT Collection)

Fw 190D-9

Intended as an interim fighter solution pending arrival of the Ta 152, Focke-Wulf always saw the Fw 190D-9 being delivered in limited numbers only, and with the minimum changes in design in order to abate costs. As the company noted in its description of the aircraft in December 1943:

The Fw 190D-9 single-seat fighter was built as a result of a requirement to install a Jumo 213A in the Fw 190A-8 airframe with the minimum possible modifications to the fuselage. It is intended that the Jumo 213A standard powerplant should be widely used. No engine-mounted cannon has been fitted, although the engine is designed to allow the later installation of the MK 108 [but not the MK 103!]. For reasons of stability, a 500mm [19.6in] section has been fitted in the rear fuselage. This partly compensates for the aircraft's nose-heaviness resulting from the installation of the heavier engine. Depending on the equipment installed in the aircraft, 10kg [22lb] to 30kg [66lb] of ballast has to be affixed in the vertical stabiliser.

The fuselage of the D-9 was essentially similar to that of the Fw 190A-8, although some changes were necessary as a result of the different engine mounting. These included the strengthening of the engine attachment fittings and the bulkhead behind them because of the considerable increase in engine attachment forces, and the aforementioned 19.6in fuselage extension intended to compensate for the lengthened engine area compared to that of the BMW 801. The longer nose was found to have a very destabilising effect on flight characteristics, especially on directional stability. The fuselage extension accommodated oxygen bottles, which were moved to the rear for centre of gravity reasons. The rear fuselage was also strengthened because the extension resulted in a considerable increase in fuselage moment (bending). This involved the installation of steel sections in some areas where Dural had previously been used.

The electrically operated undercarriage was the same as that fitted to the Fw 190A-8 and A-9. The mainwheels were 27.5in x 7in.

Control linkages remained essentially unchanged from the Fw 190A-8, although the extended rear fuselage made it necessary to lengthen the control rods. Likewise, the wing was taken from Fw 190 production and was unchanged, apart from between the wheel covers where the bottom engine support strut was deleted.

The engine bearers were taken from the Ju 188, which allowed a suitable location of the engine in terms of centre of gravity and other design factors. Accessibility at the air intake was, however, restricted by a curved support strut. In order to keep the engine mounting as short as possible, without having to mount the engine so high as

On 1 January 1945, Leutnant Theo Nibel of 10./JG 54 participated in the infamous Operation *Bodenplatte*, which saw Allied airfields attacked at dawn – Nibel's unit targeted B.60 Grimbergen, in Belgium. His Sorau-built D-9, Wk-Nr. 210079 'Black 12', suffered a bird strike and he was forced to land near Wemmel. Nibel's 'Dora' would be the first D-9 to be captured by the Allies. Here, the engine cover panels have been lifted to reveal the Jumo 213 cradled by its bearers, as well as the auxiliary coolant tank (forward) and oil tank (to the rear). (EN-Archive)

Fw 190D-9 MACHINE GUNS

The Fw 190D-9 fielded a pair of fuselage-mounted, belt-fed, air-cooled Rheinmetall-Borsig 13mm MG 131 machine guns firing at a rate of 900 rounds per minute (475 rounds per gun). The ammunition containers for the machine guns were located directly beneath the weapons.

to hamper visibility, with the agreement of Jumo, the two fuel filters were relocated to the engine underside. The engines were delivered unmodified and were adjusted by Focke-Wulf during installation. The exhaust system consisted of conventional exhaust stubs.

Two semi-circular coolant radiators were mounted around the reduction gear casing in a circular cowling, to the rear of which were annular gills, automatically controlled by a thermostat mounted at the top of the engine crankcase. The gills could be adjusted alternatively by a control in the cockpit. An air duct conveyed air via a pipe to a box around the rearward-facing exhaust stubs on each side – thence air passed through ducts in the leading edge of the wings to provide warm air for gun heating. The two 'L'-shaped coolant header tanks were mounted on either side of the engine, with the starboard tank incorporating a thermostatic relief valve. The tanks were of 13-litre capacity each and were interconnected, the starboard tank feeding into the coolant pump.

Armament fitted to the first production D-9 Wk-Nr. 210001 TR+SA comprised two 13mm MG 131 machine guns mounted over the Jumo 213A engine and two 20mm MG 151/20E cannon in the wing roots. (EN-Archive)

The aircraft was fitted with a three-bladed Junkers VS 111 constant-speed hydraulic variable-pitch propeller. Its laminated-wood blades were fitted with balance weights on each blade housing.

Two 87–90 octane self-sealing tanks were installed in the fuselage, with the forward tank holding 230 litres and the aft tank 290 litres (totalling 520 litres). There were two interconnected oil tanks of 35 litres and 25 litres at the rear of the engine on the port side. Oil was fed from the lower tank to the pressure pump on the engine. It was collected by a scavenger pump and delivered to the oil cooler, passing through the latter to a metal, disc-type, dual filter, the elements of which could be rotated by means of a lever. From the filter the oil was returned to the top oil tank, thus completing the circuit. The oil cooler, through which the coolant passed, was of the cylindrical type.

Standard armament for the D-9 comprised two 13mm MG 131s with 475 rounds per gun in the fuselage and two 20mm MG 151s with 250 rounds per gun in the wing roots. The spacing between the two MG 131s had to be increased from 10.2in to 12.1in on account of the position of the synchroniser on the Jumo 213. Recent research has revealed that there were variations in the shape of the aerodynamically streamlined cowling designed to cover the MG 131 fuselage guns. The cowling was designed to be opened using four fastening clips, and was hinged to raise upwards just in front of the canopy windscreen.

The other engine cowlings were Junkers-made, and part of the overall 'power egg' – they featured a gentle bulge at the rear to house the MG 131's electrical ammunition feed mechanism, but eventually this became unnecessary. Nevertheless, sub-contractors and satellite factories such as Weserflug (Arb. Roland), Mimetall and Fieseler produced

Fw 190D-9 CANNON

The Fw 190D-9 was also armed with a pair of Mauser 20mm MG 151/20E wing-mounted, recoil-operated, belt-fed cannon firing at a rate of 780 rounds per minute (250 rounds per gun). One weapon was mounted in each wing root, with their ammunition containers being housed just forward of the cockpit.

their own versions of the cowling in front of the windscreen, which varied in the number of panels used in construction, their 'bulges' and flairs.

Most other equipment was taken from the A-8 series, with minor changes associated mainly with the installation of the Jumo 213.

Fw 190D-9 Wk-Nr. 600375 of III./JG 26, photographed near Celle after its capture by the British. Note the oleo leg covers have been removed. (EN-Archive)

Tempest V and Fw 190D-9 Comparison Specifications		
	Tempest V	**Fw 190D-9**
Powerplant	2,180hp Napier Sabre II	1,726hp Junkers Jumo 213A
Dimensions		
Span	41ft 0in	34ft 5in
Length	33ft 8in	33ft 5.5in
Height	16ft 1in	11ft 0in
Wing area	302sq ft	196.99sq ft
Weights		
Empty	9,250lb	7,694lb
Loaded	11,400lb	9,413lb
Performance		
Max Speed	432mph at 18,400ft	440mph at 36,000ft
Range	740 miles	519 miles
Rate of Climb	4,700ft per minute	3,300ft per minute
Service Ceiling	36,500ft	39,370ft
Armament	4 x 20mm Hispano Mk II cannon 2 x 500lb or 1,000lb bombs	2 x 13mm MG 131 machine guns 2 x 20mm MG 151/20E cannon 1 x 1,102lb bomb

THE STRATEGIC SITUATION

On 6 June 1944 Allied forces landed on the coast of Normandy, pouring 155,000 men, supported by vehicles and armour, onto the beaches. The air cover for what had been codenamed Operation *Overlord* was immense, with sufficient capability to fly more than 14,500 sorties within the first 24 hours. A major component of the Allied air armada was provided by the 2nd Tactical Air Force (2nd TAF) under the command of Air Marshal Sir Arthur Coningham, a successful and highly insightful tactical air commander who had carved himself a formidable and competent reputation as leader of the Western Desert Air Force in 1942. 2nd TAF had come into existence in Britain on 15 November 1943, having been previously named simply the Tactical Air Force. Its employment would focus on providing tactical air support to the Allied armies as they advanced into France and on towards the Low Countries and, ultimately, Germany.

On the eve of *Overlord*, 2nd TAF comprised four groups made up of 85 squadrons of Spitfire, Mosquito and Tempest V fighters, Typhoon fighter-bombers and Wellington, Boston and Mitchell tactical bombers, plus support aircraft and 14 assigned transport squadrons. The Tempest V element consisted of Nos. 3 and 486 (Royal New Zealand Air Force – RNZAF) Sqns, which together formed the first Tempest wing, No. 150, led by ace Wg Cdr Roland Beamont. His was a judicious selection, for Beamont had previously served as a test pilot assigned to Hawker, where he had been involved in testing both the Typhoon and the Tempest.

In turn, No. 150 Wing was assigned to No. 85 Group (which contained all the latest air superiority fighters, including Griffon-engined Spitfire XIVs), with its two Tempest squadrons based at Newchurch near the Kent coast. The relatively small

number of Tempests – still a largely untried aircraft – were to be operated as air superiority fighters over the invasion beachhead area and as fast, defensive interceptors over southern England in the ongoing battle against the V1 flying bomb. The impact of the Tempest V on D-Day and the 24 hours that followed was muted, and its appearance went largely unnoticed by the meagre numbers of Luftwaffe aircraft that were operational. The Tempests were confined to conducting reconnaissance and convoy patrols, but on D+2 came its baptism of fire when aircraft from No. 3 Sqn, covered by No. 486 Sqn, led by Beamont spotted a flight of five Bf 109s east of Rouen. Although Beamont's aircraft was damaged in the ensuing combat, three of the Messerschmitts were shot down.

However, the Tempests were soon pulled back from air combat to deal with the growing V1 threat over southern England, a challenge which they met as part of the Air Defence of Great Britain (ADGB) with an exemplary record over the next four months.

But the Tempest's time in northwest Europe was to come. By late September 1944, the battle for France had been won by the Allies and German forces were pulling back into northeastern Belgium and the Netherlands with a grim inevitability. The Luftwaffe, in the face of dwindling resources while trying to fight a multi-front war in the south, east and west, as well as defending the airspace over the homeland against the Allied strategic bomber offensive, was being slowly bled dry in terms of pilots and fuel.

Nevertheless, the *Oberkommando der Luftwaffe* (OKL – Operations Staff) still saw the *Jagdwaffe*'s prime mission in September 1944 as one of air defence, ensuring 'domination of the air over friendly territory and the destruction of enemy aircraft by day and night.' In reality, before 'domination' could be achieved, a more immediate goal was 'equality', and even on that count the *Jagdwaffe* was substantially outgunned by Allied air strength. However, new aircraft types were under development in the

Pilots of No. 486 Sqn gather for a discussion on the grass shortly after their arrival at B.60 Grimbergen in late September 1944. The unit was part of No. 122 Wing, which also included Nos. 3 and 56 Sqns, forming a major part of the Tempest strike force in northwest Europe. Just days after this photograph was taken, the wing would move to B.80 Volkel, from where it would prosecute a relentless campaign of aerial attrition against the Luftwaffe. Seen here at far right leaning against the wheel arch of the vehicle in the foreground is No. 486 Sqn's CO, Sqn Ldr J. H. Iremonger. (CT Collection)

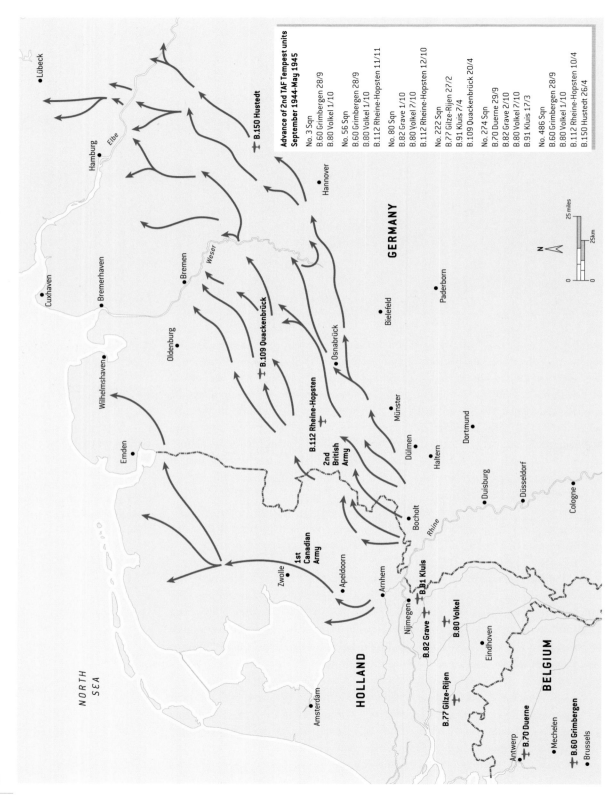

NORTH SEA

HOLLAND

GERMANY

BELGIUM

• Lübeck

• Hamburg

Elbe

• Cuxhaven

• Bremerhaven

• Bremen

Weser

• Hannover

• Oldenburg

✈ **B.109 Quackenbrück**

• Wilhelmshaven

• Emden

• Osnabrück

✈ **B.112 Rheine-Hopsten**

• Bielefeld

• Paderborn

• Münster

• Dülmen

2nd British Army

• Haltern

• Dortmund

• Zwolle

1st Canadian Army

• Apeldoorn

• Bocholt

• Duisburg

• Düsseldorf

Rhine

• Cologne

• Arnhem

• Nijmegen

✈ **B.91 Kluis**

✈ **B.82 Grave**

✈ **B.80 Volkel**

✈ **B.77 Gilze-Rijen**

• Eindhoven

✈ **B.70 Duerne**

• Antwerp

• Mechelen

✈ **B.60 Grimbergen**

• Brussels

• Amsterdam

✈ **B.150 Hustedt**

N

0 — 25 miles
0 — 25 km

Advance of 2nd TAF Tempest units September 1944-May 1945

No. 3 Sqn
B.60 Grimbergen 28/9
B.80 Volkel 1/10

No. 56 Sqn
B.60 Grimbergen 28/9
B.80 Volkel 1/10
B.112 Rheine-Hopsten 11/11

No. 80 Sqn
B.82 Grave 1/10
B.80 Volkel 7/10
B.112 Rheine-Hopsten 12/10

No. 222 Sqn
B.77 Gilze-Rijen 27/2
B.91 Kluis 7/4
B.109 Quackenbrück 20/4

No. 274 Sqn
B.70 Duerne 29/9
B.82 Grave 2/10
B.80 Volkel 7/10
B.91 Kluis 17/3

No. 486 Sqn
B.60 Grimbergen 28/9
B.80 Volkel 1/10
B.112 Rheine-Hopsten 10/4
B.150 Hustedt 26/4

Reich's factories, including the next generation of high-speed, high-altitude piston-engined fighters, including the Fw 190D-9, and the revolutionary Me 262 jet-powered interceptor. The Allies could not afford to ignore such determination on the part of the OKL, or the quality still being manufactured by German aircraft and engine firms.

Having remained in England with ADGB into the autumn of 1944, the Tempest squadrons found themselves too far away from the fluid frontlines of the Western Front by late September. So, on the 28th of that month, Nos. 3 and 486 Sqns, along with No. 56 'Punjab' Sqn, which had begun to convert from Spitfire IXs to Tempests in June, relocated from No. 150 Wing's base at Matlaske, in Norfolk, to B.60 Grimbergen in Belgium. The Hawker fighters swapped places with RAF Mustang IIIs of No. 122 Wing, Wg Cdr Beamont simultaneously taking over command of the wing from Wg Cdr W. W. J. Loud.

That very day, 250 miles to the east, another portentous event took place when Knight's Cross-holder Hauptmann Robert Weiss, the *Gruppenkommandeur* of III./JG 54 at Oldenburg, in northern Germany, took off in his new Fw 190D-9 – one of the first four such machines delivered to an operational unit – just as No. 150 Wing was preparing to move to B.60. Weiss had been ordered into the air with his wingman to intercept a lone enemy aircraft reported to be over Bremen. A short while later Weiss spotted the Spitfire PR XI

Ace Wg Cdr Roland Beamont, who had both operational and test flying experience of Typhoons and had also taken part in Tempest development, was chosen to lead No. 150 Wing – the first to be equipped with the Tempest V. (CT Collection)

flown by Flt Lt Duncan McCuaig of No. 541 Sqn, closed in with his 'Dora' and shot it down. McCuaig attempted unsuccessfully to bail out, and his aircraft crashed near the village of Apelstedt, southeast of Bremen. It was Weiss' 120th aerial victory, and the first to be credited to the Fw 190D-9. Despite some initial scepticism on the part of III./JG 54's pilots over the new Focke-Wulf, it was a promising event to have occurred within eight days of the unit taking delivery of the type.

Just nine days later, on the morning of 29 September, patrolling Tempest Vs of No. 56 Sqn led by Sqn Ldr D. V. C. 'Digger' Cotes-Preedy arrived in a timely fashion in the Emmerich-Nijmegen area to come to the aid of eight rocket-firing Typhoons of No. 137 Sqn out on an armed reconnaissance sortie. Pilots from the latter unit had started to attack an enemy motorised column when they were bounced by around 20 Bf 109s and short-nosed Fw 190s. Joining Spitfire IXs of No. 416 Sqn, the Tempests claimed five Fw 190s shot down plus a probable, with kills being credited to Cotes-Preedy and Canadian Flg Off David Ness (two) and Flg Off J. J. Payton (two) – the latter two subsequently became aces.

Within the space of ten days, the air war over northwest Europe had seen the arrival of two formidable and opposing new air superiority fighters. Their respective appearances must have given both sides a jolt, but for the Luftwaffe in particular it was another ominous harbinger.

Until December, the only Luftwaffe unit to operate the D-9 was III./JG 54. The *Gruppe* had been in the West since February 1943 when it had arrived from the USSR as part of an intended swap with elements of JG 26 which were to move east – a plan

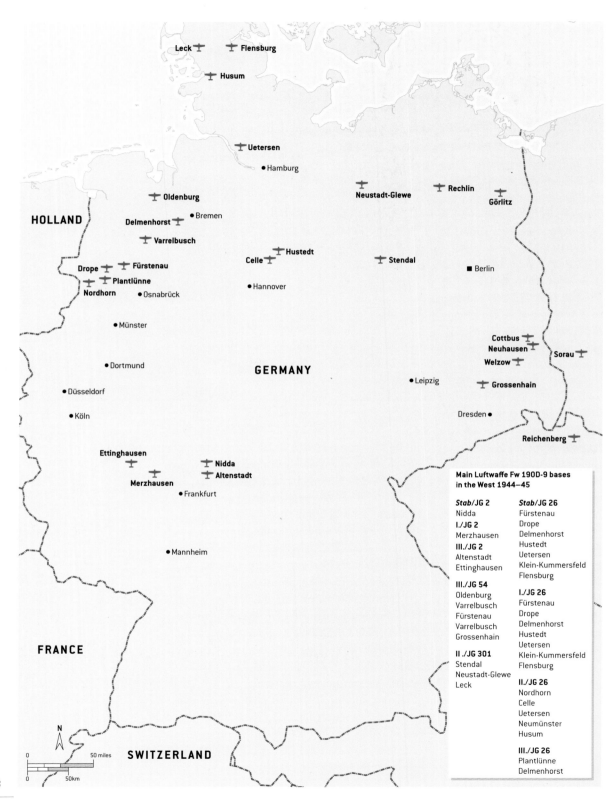

Leck ✈ ✈ Flensburg

Husum ✈

Uetersen ✈

• Hamburg

HOLLAND

Oldenburg ✈

✈ Neustadt-Glewe ✈ Rechlin

✈ Görlitz

Delmenhorst ✈ • Bremen

Varrelbusch ✈

Celle ✈ ✈ Hustedt

✈ Stendal

Drope ✈ ✈ Fürstenau

■ Berlin

✈ Plantlünne

Nordhorn • Osnabrück

• Hannover

• Münster

GERMANY

Cottbus ✈
Neuhausen ✈
Welzow ✈   Sorau ✈

• Dortmund

• Leipzig

✈ Grossenhain

• Düsseldorf

• Köln

Dresden •

Reichenberg ✈

Ettinghausen ✈
                 ✈ Nidda
Merzhausen ✈   ✈ Altenstadt

• Frankfurt

• Mannheim

FRANCE

N

0 _____ 50 miles
0 _____ 50km

SWITZERLAND

**Main Luftwaffe Fw 190D-9 bases
in the West 1944–45**

Stab/JG 2
Nidda
I./JG 2
Merzhausen
III./JG 2
Altenstadt
Ettinghausen

III./JG 54
Oldenburg
Varrelbusch
Fürstenau
Varrelbusch
Grossenhain

II./JG 301
Stendal
Neustadt-Glewe
Leck

Stab/JG 26
Fürstenau
Drope
Delmenhorst
Hustedt
Uetersen
Klein-Kummersfeld
Flensburg

I./JG 26
Fürstenau
Drope
Delmenhorst
Hustedt
Uetersen
Klein-Kummersfeld
Flensburg

II./JG 26
Nordhorn
Celle
Uetersen
Neumünster
Husum

III./JG 26
Plantlünne
Delmenhorst

that was never entirely executed. III./JG 54's initial duties had been the air defence of the coastlines of northern France while based at Vendeville and then, from late March 1943, of the north German coast from Oldenburg. From June 1943 until May 1944, the *Gruppe* engaged in similar duties over the Dutch coast, in addition to patrolling German waters, until it received orders to relocate to Illesheim in May 1944 for operations in defence of the Reich. Then with the Allied invasion of Normandy, the *Gruppe*'s Fw 190A-8s were among just under 1,000 fighters that hastily arrived in France from Germany – these aircraft were drawn from JG 1, JG 3, JG 11, JG 27, JG 77 and JG 301. The aircraft were rushed to a 60-mile-long belt of airfields running parallel to the Channel coast constructed by *Luftflotte* 3, with III./JG 54 locating to Villacoublay.

Operating from barely prepared emergency strips, the German fighters struggled throughout June and July to make even a dent in the overwhelming Allied strength. As early as mid-June, *Luftflotte* 3 had lost 75 per cent of the strength it possessed immediately prior to the landings, and the units in France were plagued by technical problems, accidents and supply issues. The Allied air forces constantly strafed and bombed the French airfields, and a new pilot, lacking in training and flying time, was lucky to survive more than three sorties.

To make matters worse for III./JG 54, the unit's *Gruppenkommandeur*, 102-victory ace Major Werner Schroer, was suddenly taken ill and command was passed to Hauptmann Weiss, who had transferred from I. *Gruppe*. Throughout the summer of 1944, III./JG 54 fought doggedly over France, but by mid-August, having suffered accumulating losses, the *Gruppe* was operating with a minimum number of pilots. On the 15th it was withdrawn from Normandy and assigned as the first unit to receive the new, much vaunted 'Dora'.

The first four examples arrived at Oldenburg from Rechlin on 20 September, but initial reaction amongst the pilots of III./JG 54 was sceptical. Pilots expressed their concerns over the extended fuselage and the new, heavier Jumo engine when compared to the shorter Fw 190A-8 and its BMW powerplant. However, that afternoon, once Weiss and his four *Staffelkapitäne* had flown the '*Langnase*' with its superior turn and fast rate of climb, opinions changed for the better.

Two more D-9s were delivered on the 26th, and when Weiss shot down Flt Lt McCuaig's Spitfire PR XI two days later, it seemed like a good omen. Then, on the 30th, no less a figure than Dipl.-Ing. Professor Kurt Tank visited Oldenburg, and both

By early 1945, the Luftwaffe could not afford to allow its fighters to remain open to attack on airfields with no concealment or protection. In a scene common all over Germany, Fw 190D-9s of 7./JG 26, led at the time by Oberleutnant Gottfried Schmidt, emerge from their wooded dispersal at Nordhorn-Klausheide for another patrol in February 1945. (EN-Archive)

designer and pilots had the opportunity to discuss issues related to the new fighter. Tank explained that the D-9 should be regarded as an interim fighter intended to take advantage of the availability of the Jumo 213 following a decrease in demand for the engine in bombers, production of which had been drastically curtailed after priority was given to fighters.

September did indeed see record deliveries of more than 3,000 new or repaired single-engined fighters. By October, new, improved types were reaching the units. For example, III./JG 27 at Köln-Wahn took delivery of the first 75 enhanced and aerodynamically refined Bf 109K-4s. By the end of September, 30 Fw 190D-9s were available for service, and during October a further 68 aircraft had been delivered.

The immediate problem facing the *Jagdwaffe* was a lack of sufficiently trained pilots able to defend the skies over the Reich or the Western Front. However, the situation on the ground in the West had so deteriorated by this stage that neither Generalfeldmarschall Walter Model, the Supreme Commander in-theatre, or his replacement, Gerd von Rundstedt, were able to stem the rapid pace of the Allied advance. By late October, Field Marshal Bernard Montgomery's troops and armour had reached the southern banks of the Scheldt, where their task was to flush the estuary of resistance so as to open Antwerp to Allied shipping. In mid-September, and further to the east, the first American troops had crossed the Sauer north of Trier and penetrated the frontier of the Reich itself. Two weeks later, elements of the American First Army breached what was thought to be the impenetrable Siegfried Line north of Aachen. The Front was collapsing, and the Allies were now fighting within the borders of the Reich.

Meanwhile, as the dismal autumn of 1944 progressed, more *Gruppen* began to receive the D-9. On 7 November, II./JG 26 at Kirchhellen, under the command of Major Anton Hackl, was informed that it was to move to Reinsehlen to transition to the 'Dora', with some pilots collecting aircraft at Helmstedt and then flying them to the new base for training. The *Gruppe* was assigned 55 Fw 190D-9s in December, but by the middle of the month there was growing pressure being placed on the unit from its tactical command, II. *Jagdkorps*, to quicken training. On the 14th Bf 109s from III. *Gruppe* were attacked by Tempest Vs from No. 56 Sqn while on a covering mission for Me 262 jet bombers at Rheine and three of the Messerschmitt fighters were shot down. On the 17th, II./JG 26 moved into Nordhorn-Klausheide with 74 D-9s and 20 freshly trained aviators amongst its pilot cadre.

At Stendal, Hauptmann Herbert Nölter's II./JG 301 had received its first D-9s in early December, and I. and III./JG 2 under Hauptmanns Franz Hrdlicka and Siegfried Lemke, respectively, took delivery of 12 Fw 190D-9s in the middle of the month, with 53 'Doras' in place at III. *Gruppe's* base at Ettinghausen towards the end of it.

Hauptmann Franz Hrdlicka was made *Gruppenkommandeur* of I./JG 2 on 1 December 1944, and a fortnight later his unit received 12 brand new Fw 190D-9s. A recipient of the Knight's Cross, he had claimed at least 43 victories with 5./JG 77 during the course of some 500 missions over the Eastern and Italian fronts prior to joining I./JG 2. Credited with the destruction of a B-26 in the 'Dora', Hrdlicka was shot down and killed by USAAF fighters on 25 March 1945. (EN-Archive)

THE COMBATANTS

RAF PILOT TRAINING

The Tempest V was, without doubt, an excellent aeroplane in all respects, but its size and power meant that it required properly trained, competent handling. Most pilots found it responsive, although it could be tricky on take-off. As the Tempest represented the cutting edge of piston-engined aircraft development in Britain in the mid-war years, it became critical that pilots were well trained.

Much of the responsibility – and success – in training the huge numbers of aircrew during the war rested in the Empire Air Training Scheme (later known as the British Commonwealth Air Training Plan). Commencing in April 1940, this ambitious programme had its origins in the pre-war recognition that facilities in Britain, as a relatively small, potentially vulnerable island, would be entirely unsuitable for the efficient and safe training of pilots and aircrew. In the Dominions, however, there were vast spaces and safe skies. RAF historian Sir Maurice Dean considered the scheme, 'one of the most brilliant pieces of imaginative organisation ever conceived.'

By 1943, at its peak, between them, the Empire air forces and the USA mustered 333 flying training schools across Great Britain (still by far the most), Canada (92), Australia (26), South Africa (25), Southern Rhodesia (10), India (9), New Zealand (6), the Middle East (6), USA (5) and the Bahamas (1). Between 1940–45, the scheme trained 293,604 airmen, with, additionally, more than 14,000 in the USA as part of the Arnold Scheme. Of this total, 110,600 were pilots.

Canada had the second highest number of schools because of its unlimited space for the development of airfields and considerable industrial potential that could be turned to the manufacture of aircraft and other equipment. In addition, it was close to the resources of the USA. When British trainee pilots arrived in Canada they found conditions to be like another world. 'It is like coming into paradise here,' one wrote home in July 1942. 'Food served at the camp is marvellous – all the butter, sugar, milk you want. The people too are marvellously hospitable.'

In Britain, potential pilot candidates progressed through several stages of training, which started with eight weeks of ground instruction covering subjects such as mathematics, navigation and the principles of flying. Ten weeks' basic training was carried out at an Elementary Flying Training School (EFTS), where students learnt the basics of flying an aircraft with an instructor, often in a two-seat de Havilland DH.82 Tiger Moth in which they would also make their first solo flight.

More advanced training would follow for 16 weeks at a Service Flying Training School (SFTS), where pupils would simultaneously continue further classroom instruction, being drilled in aerial navigation, night and formation flying exercises, and undergo simulation flying or Link training. They were also familiarized with more powerful aircraft such as the North American Harvard I/II. At the conclusion of the school course, final tests and examinations would be taken and, if successful, the newly qualified pilot would receive his 'wings'.

A similar route was taken in Canada, as experienced by future Typhoon pilot J. B. Friedlander from Montreal. After leaving university, Friedlander enlisted in the RAF, being funnelled through the Initial Training Wing and EFTS at Portage-la-Prairie in Manitoba. At the EFTS, trainees received around 50 hours of single-engined aircraft flying time and aeronautical theory. Friedlander flew Tiger Moths, soloing after eight hours, and at the SFTS he flew Harvards, receiving his wings in April 1942. Eventually arriving in England in September 1943, he undertook Link Trainer exercises in Bournemouth before moving to an Operational Training Unit (OTU), where he learned to fly the Miles Master III two-seat advanced trainer, as well as Spitfires and Hurricanes. 'I never did like the Master,' Friedlander recalled, 'which seemed to blow around like a fart in a mitten.' Friedlander went on to fly 175 hours on Typhoons, completing 120 operational sorties and being awarded the Distinguished Flying Cross (DFC).

RAF student pilots learning to fly in Canada would progress on to the Harvard II at one of a number of SFTSs spread across the country. Typically, they would spend 16 weeks here, receiving their 'wings' as newly qualified pilots upon the successful completion of this advanced phase of their course. Harvard II AJ966 was delivered new to No. 39 SFTS at Swift Current, Saskatchewan, in early 1942. It had been transferred to No. 37 STFS at Calgary, Alberta, by the time this photograph was taken, and the Harvard was destroyed in a crash near Midnapore, Alberta, on 31 December 1943. (Philip Jarrett Collection)

Englishman Ronald Appleby, who would eventually fly 114 sorties in Typhoons with No. 181 Sqn and be awarded the DFC on 8 May 1945, spent time at several flying schools in the USA from May 1942. Having completed ground school following a 'dreary period of waiting', he was eventually sent to the civilian-run Darr Aero Tech flying school in Albany, Georgia, followed by others in Alabama and Florida. Appleby returned to Britain as a pilot in December 1942, where, after more waiting, he was posted in

An American civilian instructor shows RAF cadets the controls in the cockpit of a Boeing-Stearman PT-17 Kaydet at Carlstrom Field in Arcadia, Florida. All Arnold Scheme flying training of British and Commonwealth student pilots at this site was overseen by the Riddle Aeronautical Institute. Carlstrom was one of seven sites in the Southeast Air Corps Training Center area to provide Primary flying courses (that lasted up to ten weeks) for RAF pilots. USAAC and RAF instructors would replace their civilian counterparts for the Basic and Advanced phases of the Arnold Scheme. (NARA)

May 1943 to Typhoon-equipped No. 55 OTU at Annan, in Dumfrieshire. Here, much time was spent discussing the challenges of flying the Typhoon, and its technical shortcomings, to the point where students were told that if they misbehaved on course they would be posted to a Typhoon squadron as punishment!

Also training at Darr Aero Tech was E. A. 'Fin' Haddock from Newcastle who, after attending the EFTS at Babbacombe, in Devon, sailed across the Atlantic to Canada, via Iceland, avoiding U-boats along the way. It took 'Fin' three days to travel from the snow and ice of Canada to the sun and warmth of Georgia, where he trained up on the two-seat Boeing-Stearman PT-17 Kaydet biplane. Haddock enjoyed a good working relationship with his instructor until the time came to go solo, as he recalled:

For some reason, I couldn't see the need to apply right rudder to keep the nose of the PT-17 fixed in a straight line. His [the instructor's] answer was to cut the engine as soon as I got airborne, apply the brakes and a quick taxi back to my starting point, with a curt 'Do it again.' After half-a-dozen attempts he said, 'Okay, off you go,' and I went off on my first solo. Luckily, all went well.

The Stearman was twice the size of a Tiger Moth, and, with its 220hp Continental R-670 radial engine, made an ideal trainer. Another regularly used basic training aircraft in America was the Vultee BT-13 Valiant.

During the early stages of the war, a pilot could be trained sufficiently in as little as six months or 150 flying hours, but as the war progressed and aircraft became more sophisticated, on average it took between 18 months and two years, or around 200–320 flying hours. From 1941 onwards, the training syllabus was reviewed. Changes in operational procedure required additional training, while the development of more modern aircraft meant a higher standard of flying technique and piloting skill was needed. While training could not be rushed, time was always a pressurising factor and instructors were constantly pushed to revise and shorten courses wherever possible.

TEMPEST V COCKPIT

1. Airspeed indicator
2. Artificial horizon
3. Rate of climb indicator
4. Altimeter
5. Direction indicator
6. Turn and bank indicator
7. Flap lever
8. Hydraulic hand pump
9. Radiator shutter lever
10. Gunsight control and weapons selector box
11. Undercarriage lever
12. Supercharger lever
13. Throttle friction wheel
14. Throttle lever
15. Canopy winding handle
16. Reading lamp switch
17. Undercarriage emergency release switch
18. Undercarriage indicator lights
19. Beam approach button
20. Magneto switches
21. Cut-out safety control

22. Propeller pitch lever
23. Punkah louvre (late-build aircraft)
24. Watch holder
25. Wheel brake pressure indicator
26. T.R. 1143 transmitter and receiver control unit
27. Undercarriage indicators
28. Oxygen delivery indicator
29. Oxygen supply indicator
30. Contactor switch
31. Engine starting boost coil switch
32. Engine starter switch
33. Remote contactor
34. Flap position indicator
35. Reflector gunsight on/off switch
36. Cockpit light switch (port)
37. Armoured windscreen
38. Gunsight (Type I Mk 1, reflected from windscreen)
39. Spare bulbs for gunsight

40. Cockpit light switch (starboard)
41. Compass light switch
42. Rev counter
43. Compass card
44. Oil pressure indicator
45. Fuel pressure indicator light
46. Hood jettison lever
47. Power failure warning light
48. Boost gauge
49. Fuel contents gauge (main tank)
50. Oil temperature indicator
51. Fuel contents gauge (wing tanks)
52. Radiator temperature indicator
53. Punkah louvre (late-build aircraft)
54. Cockpit heating lever
55. Very pistol opening
56. Fuel tank pressure lever
57. Fuel cocks (inter, main and nose tanks)
58. Cylinder priming pump

59. Engine data card
60. Signalling switch box
61. Windscreen anti-icing pumps
62. Carburettor priming pump
63. Very pistol cartridge stowage
64. Pressure head heating switch
65. T.R. 1143 master switch
66. Heated clothing switch
67. Dimmer switch
68. Voltmeter
69. Navigation light switch
70. Risin switch
71. Gun camera master switch
72. Pilot's seat and cushion
73. Cartridge starter reload handle
74. Gun button
75. Control column
76. Radio button
77. Compass
78. Rudder Bar
79. Elevator trim wheel
80. Rudder trim wheel
81. External stores salvo switch

Schools were also frequently required to increase the size of their intakes, resulting in problems with the supply of equipment and a shortage of instructors.

In January 1941 the British government asked the RNZAF to reduce the length of its training courses. This request was rejected because many instructors were relatively inexperienced, having only recently graduated from Flying Instructors' School, and it was felt that they could not cope successfully with the training of pupils if courses were shortened still further. Secondly, aircraft and spare parts were still in short supply, and the problems of keeping machines serviceable would intensify, placing further burden on already overworked maintenance personnel.

Despite such factors, by 1943 there was a surplus of trained pilots. Indeed, in Canada at the beginning of July 1944 there were 400 New Zealand pilots awaiting training who, it was estimated, would not be absorbed into the system before December. It was therefore decided that no more would be required in Canada until May 1945.

The training process had become refined in Britain by 1944, with a first phase of initial training comprising reporting to an Aircrew Reception Centre (six weeks), at the end of which aircrew candidates would be graded at the EFTS (three weeks). They would then be assigned to an appropriate Initial Training Wing (eight weeks), which marked the conclusion of the first phase. The second phase of elementary training commenced with reporting to an Aircrew Despatch Centre, where the time spent could vary depending on the competence of the trainee and the complexity of the training. Trainees then returned to the EFTS for ten weeks, before moving on to the third phase of advanced training. This commenced with 20 weeks at SFTS, culminating in the presentation of wings, followed by a period at a Personnel Despatch Centre, then six weeks at a Personnel Reception/Receiving Centre, before moving on

The New Zealanders of No. 122 Wing gather for a 'team photo' in front of one of their Tempest Vs at B.80 Volkel over Christmas 1944. In the front row, sixth from left, is Flt Lt K. F. Thiele of No. 3 Sqn, seventh is Sqn Ldr 'Spike' Umbers of No. 486 Sqn, eighth is Sqn Ldr E. D. Mackie of No. 274 Sqn, tenth is Sqn Ldr R. L. Spurdle of No. 80 Sqn and eleventh is Flt Lt H. A. Crafts of No. 274 Sqn. No. 486 Sqn pilots Flg Offs Keith Smith (far left on wing), Ray Danzey (far right on wing) and Sid Short (standing far left) and Plt Off Jimmy Sheddan (standing fourth from left) took part in the Tempest V's first ever engagement with Fw 190D-9s of III./JG 54 on 27 December 1944. (CT Collection)

to an Aircrew Officer or NCO Course for four weeks. Upon completion, fighter pilots would then receive four to six weeks' instruction at an Advanced Flying Unit, before being posted to an OTU, where they would spend nine weeks preparing for operational and frontline service.

However, even after having been assigned to squadron service, an experienced pilot would be recalled for specialist training courses to keep him fully briefed on new developments in aircraft design, navigation, weapons and changes in operational procedure.

Tempest V EJ809/GF-X was assigned to a flight within No. 56 OTU, a unit established in early 1943 at Tealing, in Angus, Scotland, for the training of pilots destined to fly single-engined fighters in the frontline. The flight specialised in the instruction of low-level navigation. On 5 October 1943, No. 56 OTU was re-designated No. 1 Combat Training Wing to provide specialist tactical and weapons training to pilots who had completed their standard operational training, although a No. 56 OTU was also retained for the training of Typhoon and Tempest pilots. Seen here standing beside GF-X is unit instructor Flt Lt C. Ivan Smith. (CT Collection)

This was the route by which scores of pilots found themselves sitting in the cockpit of the Tempest V.

LUFTWAFFE PILOT TRAINING

The 1930s fostered a powerful sense of enthusiasm for aviation in a resurgent Germany. Thousands of young men – and many women – had been captivated by the glamour of flight. Boys grew up spellbound by the stories of Manfred von Richthofen – the famed 'Red Air Fighter' – and many other leading aces from World War I. This enthusiasm was fuelled further when Adolf Hitler rose to power in January 1933. He recognised the tremendous propaganda and potential military value in sports flying and duly formed the *Nationalsozialistiches Fliegerkorps*, a branch of the Nazi Party, to encourage boys from the age of 12 to take up flying. In line with this new 'air-minded' Nazi stance, youth from all over the Reich flocked to embark on courses in field craft, workshop duties, physical fitness and, ultimately, glider flying.

Typically, any boy attracted to aviation before and during the early years of the war would build model aircraft and then, if wanting to progress further, would enlist in his local 'Flying Hitler Youth' while still at school. Here, he was taught how to build and fly elementary plywood gliders such as the SG 38. Sufficiently competent, the aspiring aviator set about obtaining the required three grades of the Civil Gliding Proficiency Badge (A, B, and C) flying a Grunau Baby glider over the next five years. This involved five flights of 20 seconds each and one of 30 seconds (for A), five straight and level flights of 60 seconds (for B) and a final series of more lengthy flights (for C). Once a gliding badge had been earned, a candidate could then seriously start to contemplate service in the Luftwaffe.

One such young man was Gerhard Kroll, whose training was typical of the time and who would go on to fly the Fw 190D-9 in combat. Born in Elbing, West Prussia, on 17 September 1924, Kroll enlisted in the Luftwaffe in 1941 at the age of 17. In line with Luftwaffe policy, on 1 December 1941 Kroll was assigned to a

Fliegerausbildungsregiment (FAR – Flying Training Regiment), where future aircrew underwent basic infantry training. This lasted some six to twelve months, and also incorporated military discipline and physical culture; in Kroll's case he served with the 5. *Kompanie* of *Fliegerausbildungsregiment* 23 under Generalmajor Josef Putlar at Kaufbeuren, in the Allgäu region of southern Germany. The only aviation-related topics taught during this period were lectures on radio operation and map reading. Later in the war these courses were abbreviated to two or three months only.

Three months later after passing out from the FAR, Kroll was posted to 3. *Kompanie* of the Luftwaffe's *Fliegeranwärterbataillon* (Cadet Battalion) III based at Straubing, southeast of Regensburg, under Oberst Karl-August von Blomberg. During his time with the unit it was relocated to Vannes, in northwestern France. Here, as a recruit deemed to be suitable for flying training, Kroll studied general aeronautical subjects for two months.

Accepted for flying training, and again in line with standard Luftwaffe training policy, Kroll was posted to *Flugzeugführerschule* A/B 14 under the command of Oberstleutnant Emil Becker at Klagenfurt, in Austria, in the autumn of 1942. At *Flugzeugführerschule*, the student pilot would undertake a course to qualify for his powered aircraft certificates. The basic powered aircraft A1 certificate required that the trainee complete a loop, three landings without any errors, an altitude flight to 6,500ft and a 190-mile triangular flight course. All of these were to be accomplished in single- or two-seat aircraft weighing up to 1,100lbs.

A2 certification was similar except that it was for aircraft with at least two seats; as most pilots in the Luftwaffe trained on dual-control machines, this was the usual starter qualification. Following on from this was the B1 certificate. To obtain this, the student had to show that he had already achieved at least 1,850 miles of flight experience, completed a 370-mile triangular course in nine hours, climbed to an altitude of 15,000ft and undertaken at least 50 flights in aircraft in the B1 category (single-engined one- to three-seaters with a maximum weight of 5,500lbs). On top of

A member of the 'Flying Hitler Youth' receives tuition from a *Nationalsozialistisches Fliegerkorps* (NSFK) instructor on how to safely handle his SG 38 glider. The NSFK was a paramilitary organisation of the Nazi Party that was founded on 15 April 1937 as a successor to the *Deutscher Luftsportverband* (German Air Sports Association). (EN-Archive)

this experience, the pilot had to carry out three precision landings, two night landings and a night flight lasting at least 30 minutes. The B2 certificate was progressively more difficult, requiring 3,700 miles of flight experience (including at least 1,860 miles in B1 class aircraft). In addition, 50 further night flights were necessary, which had to include several difficult night landings.

Kroll was awarded his A/B certificates in January 1943, assigned the rank of Gefreiter

The Arado Ar 66C was just one of half-a-dozen or so small biplane types used as primary trainers by the Luftwaffe. Despite the Ar 66C being the least known of all the biplane trainers, 1,425 examples were built by Arado from 1933 and duly issued to most of the *Flugzeugführerschule* A/B. This aircraft, Wk-Nr. 2165, was assigned to FFS A/B 8 and is seen in flight over Karlsbad in June 1941. (EN-Archive)

(Private) and sent to *Jagdfliegerschule* (JFS) 1 under the leadership of Oberstleutnant Otto-Friedrich *Frhr* von Houwald at Pau, in southwestern France. Kroll's arrival at JFS 1 coincided with major changes being implemented within the Luftwaffe's fighter training infrastructure. In the spring of 1943, the *Jagdfliegerschulen,* where the trainee undertook initial fighter training and where he was allowed to fly various obsolete or foreign single-seat fighter aircraft such as the Arado Ar 68 and Heinkel He 51 biplanes, early model Bf 109s and captured French Dewoitine D.520 monoplanes, before moving to existing operational types, were put on a semi-operational footing. Ceasing to be designated as *Jagdfliegerschulen* and becoming *Jagdgeschwader* instead, JFS 1 was redesignated JG 101, with command passing to veteran fighter pilot Oberstleutnant Erich von Selle.

In the summer of 1943 Kroll was promoted to Unteroffizier and had done sufficiently well to become an instructor within the unit himself – a position he filled until January 1944, when he was posted to the *Ergänzungsgruppe* (Operational Training Group) of JG 54 at Bayonne. Training up on the Bf 109G and passing through this *Gruppe* within a matter of six or seven weeks, Kroll was posted to 9./JG 54, based at Ludwigslust and equipped with Bf 109s for operations in the *Reichsverteidigung* (Defence of the Reich) on 20 February 1944.

Thus it was that like many pilots who came to fly the D-9 in the closing months of the war, Kroll had already tasted considerable air combat. While engaging a USAAF B-17 on 8 March 1944 his Messerschmitt was hit by return fire and he was forced to bail out, spending a week on leave while he recovered from an injury to his ankle sustained when he landed by parachute. Exactly a month later, Kroll was shot down again, suffering third-degree burns when his Bf 109G crash-landed in flames. Hospitalised in Lüneburg until the end of July 1944, Kroll was posted to 1./*Jagdgruppe Ost* at Sagan, in Silesia, the following month. While here he transitioned onto the Fw 190, flying the A-4 to A-8 variants. It was during his time in Sagan that Kroll received news of the death of his father. A Luftwaffe Feldwebel at Halberstadt airfield, he had been killed in an air raid on the base. Kroll was given compassionate leave to collect his father's effects and take them home to West Prussia.

Then, on 9 September, he was reassigned to Oldenburg-based 9./JG 54 under the command of Oberleutnant Willi Heilmann, which was in the process of converting to the Fw 190D-9. It is probable that Kroll was one of the small number of pilots selected by two of III./JG 54's aces, Oberleutnant Hans Dortenmann, *Kapitän* of 12. *Staffel*, and Leutnant Peter Crump of 10. *Staffel*, who had been despatched by *Gruppenkommandeur* Hauptmann Weiss to *Jagdgruppe Ost* at Sagan to select suitable candidates to fly the new 'Dora'. Unfortunately, both Dortenmann and Crump were utterly dismayed by what they found at 1./*Jagdgruppe Ost*. The standard of training was alarmingly poor, with the student pilots lacking sufficient flying experience as a result of hurried instruction. They were thus also lacking in confidence, and in no way prepared for what lay ahead of them in the deadly skies over the Western Front.

This was symptomatic of the Luftwaffe's position by late 1944 and it was beginning to show in the air. Nevertheless, in mid-November, Reichsmarschall Hermann Göring, Supreme Commander of the Luftwaffe, had issued orders to II. *Jagdkorps* that its main tasks in the *Reichsverteidigung* were 'to attack enemy fighter-bombers at airfields near the frontline' and, even more importantly, 'to fly fighter cover for the Army to give it freedom of movement.' But the commander of the *Korps*, Generalmajor Dietrich Peltz, had become increasingly concerned as reports reached him of German fighter pilots breaking off engagements with enemy fighters without good reason and jettisoning drop tanks to race back to the relative safety of Reich airspace.

Fuel was still available in reasonable quantities for frontline units, but a shortage was beginning to impinge on the flying schools, affecting standards. By late 1944, fuel stocks for training were at their lowest levels. Standard training had been cut from 260 hours per pupil to about 50, which made it virtually impossible for even the very best instructors to produce fighter pilots capable of surviving in the frontline. In the *Ergänzungsgruppen*, only 20 tons of fuel equating to 25 hours of flying was available for each student pilot – much less than their RAF counterparts.

No two-seat Fw 190D-9s were ever built, so novice pilots destined to fly the type routinely received training in two-seat Bf 109G-12s like these machines assigned to JG 101 at Pau in March 1944. Both aircraft were almost certainly converted in the Messerschmitt factory from standard single-seat G-6s. The G-12s are still adorned with four-letter factory codes, and the aircraft in the foreground also boasts a 'trainer yellow' tail band. (EN-Archive)

Fw 190D-9 COCKPIT

1. FuG 16ZY communication and homing switch and volume control
2. FuG 16ZY receiver fine tuning
3. FuG 16ZY homing range switch
4. FuG 16ZY frequency selector switch
5. Tailplane trim switch
6. Undercarriage and landing flap actuation buttons
7. Undercarriage and landing flap position indicators
8. Throttle
9. Throttle-mounted propeller pitch control thumb switch
10. Tailplane trim indicator
11. Instrument panel lighting dimmer dial
12. Pilot's seat
13. Throttle friction knob
14. Control column
15. Bomb release button
16. Rudder pedals
17. Wing gun firing button
18. Fuel tank selector lever
19. Engine starter brushes withdrawal handle
20. Stopcock control lever
21. FuG 25a IFF control panel
22. Undercarriage manual lowering handle
23. Cockpit ventilation knob
24. Altimeter
25. Pitot tube heater light
26. MG 131 'armed' indicator lights
27. Ammunition counters
28. SZKK 4 armament switch and control panel
29. 30mm armoured glass windscreen panels
30. Windscreen spray pipes
31. 50mm armoured glass windsceen
32. Revi 16B reflector gunsight
33. Padded coaming
34. Gunsight padded mounting
35. AFN 2 homing indicator (FuG 16ZY)
36. Ultraviolet lights (port/starboard)
37. Airspeed indicator
38. Artificial horizon
39. Rate of climb/descent indicator
40. Repeater compass
41. Supercharger pressure gauge
42. Tachometer
43. Ventral stores and manual release handle
44. Fuel and oil pressure gauge
45. Oil temperature gauge
46. Coolant temperature gauge
47. Engine ventilation flap control lever
48. Fuel contents gauge
49. Propeller pitch indicator
50. Rear fuel tank switchover light (white)
51. Fuel content warning light (red)
52. Fuel gauge selector switch
53. WGr. 21cm underwing mortar control panel
54. Bomb fusing selector panel and external stores indicator lights
55. Oxygen flow indicator
56. Flare pistol holder
57. Oxygen pressure gauge
58. Oxygen flow valve
59. Canopy actuator wheel
60. Canopy jettison lever
61. Circuit breaker panel cover
62. Clock
63. Map holder
64. Operations information card
65. Flare box cover
66. Starter switch
67. Flare box cover plate release latch
68. Fuel pump circuit breaker switches
69. Compass deviation card
70. Circuit breaker panel cover
71. Armament circuit breakers
72. Windscreen washer operating lever

At III./JG 54, Weiss and his executive officers endeavoured to maintain some kind of effective training regime, particularly when bad weather curtailed flying and young pilots grew bored. If possible, daily lectures were held on tactics, including low-level attacks, gunnery and target training, flying and formation discipline and radio technique. They were also required to watch the mechanics and armourers at work so that they could obtain a real understanding of how the 'Dora' functioned.

Oberleutnant Dortenmann noted in his diary on 20 October:

Strain and fatigue appear etched on the face of Hauptmann Robert Weiss, *Gruppenkommandeur* of III./JG 54 while in France in 1944. On 28 September 1944 Weiss shot down a Spitfire PR XI of No. 541 Sqn while flying one of his *Gruppe*'s first Fw 190D-9s, and in doing so claimed the first aerial victory for the 'Dora' and took his personal tally to 120. He would be shot down and killed by a Spitfire IX from No. 331 'Norwegian' Sqn minutes after claiming his 122nd victory on 29 December 1944. (EN-Archive)

I hound my *Staffel* to fly as many practice missions as possible. We fly in any weather. They have given me freedom of action. In a short period of time I mould the *Staffel* into a fighting unit, train my *Rotten* and *Schwarm* leaders and look with a little more confidence to the future. In order that my pilots always know where their boss is I order that my aircraft's tail is painted bright yellow. That is very colourful and can be seen for a great distance. I don't care if the Americans and British will take mine to be a leader's aircraft; I have my pride too. With my little yellow tail everything works out fine. I don't have to scream my head off when the novices fly after the wrong aircraft during a diving attack, and they save themselves a dressing down after they land.

By comparison, the pilots of Major Karl Borris's I./JG 26 commenced flying the Fw 190D-9 at Fürstenau on 17 December, but they were not able to enjoy the benefit of being pulled back from the frontline to do so. Instead, they had to train in the new 'Langnase' while on full combat alert.

It was perhaps inevitable that at some point the Tempest V and the Fw 190D-9 would clash. Just before midday on 27 December 1944 at Varrelbusch airfield, a few kilometres north of Cloppenburg in northern Germany, the cold air was disturbed by the thunderous roar of some 60 Jumo 213 engines as Fw 190D-9s from III./JG 54 prepared to take off on a mission to cover the landing of a small number of Ar 234 jet bombers. The latter machines, from 9./KG 76 at Münster-Handorf, were due at Varrelbusch shortly after midday following an attack on the Ardennes front. After having completed their primary task, the D-9 pilots were to spend the rest of their time aloft familiarising themselves, in formation, with the landscape of the Münster basin so that future jet protection sorties could be flown with confidence. Flying conditions were perfect – good visibility and cloudless winter skies. At 1205 hrs, a green flare climbed into the sky above Varrelbusch and the first D-9s of 10. *Staffel* taxied out.

Some 155 miles to the west, eight Tempest Vs from No. 486 Sqn, led by Sqn Ldr K. G. Taylor-Cannon, had taken off from B.80 Volkel for a fighter sweep over the Paderborn area. At some point they were alerted from the ground to the presence of a large formation of German aircraft detected in the Münster area.

The first clash was about to take place.

EVAN MACKIE

New Zealander Evan Dall Mackie was born of Scottish descent in Waihi on the country's North Island on 31 October 1917, the fourth child of an engine driver turned gold miner. He grew up in his parents' miner's cottage and when not at school, his predominantly outdoor childhood in the small, coastal town was spent fishing, gathering wood for the fire, cycling, hiking and dancing Highland reels as his father played the pipes.

In 1939, with the likelihood of war in Europe and elsewhere in the world, Mackie felt that he would need to prepare, and enrolled on a correspondence course for prospective aircrew in the RNZAF, despite not having any particular interest in flying. Nevertheless, having done well on the course, he applied to join the RNZAF on 27 May 1940 at 22 years of age and entered service on 19 January 1941. After training at No. 4 EFTS at Whenuapai, Auckland, where he learned on Tiger Moths, Mackie headed to Canada as part of the British Commonwealth Air Training Plan. Once there, he undertook further training at Medicine Hat, Alberta, prior to joining No. 32 SFTS at Moose Jaw, Saskatchewan, where he flew Harvards – an aircraft with which Mackie was impressed as a result of its size, power and roominess.

Having crossed the Atlantic, Mackie undertook further training on Spitfires at No. 58 OTU in Grangemouth, Stirlingshire, prior to being posted to No. 485 Sqn at Kenley, in Surrey, in early 1942. Mackie confessed to some sense of unease that he would not 'measure up' to the rigours of being a fighter pilot, but on 26 March, just a few weeks after joining, he shared his first victory when he jointly shot down a Bf 109E five miles west of Le Havre with fellow future high-scoring ace Flt Lt Bill Crawford-Compton while flying a Spitfire VB.

From then on his confidence grew, and in early 1943, with an Fw 190 'probable' also to his name, he joined No. 243 Sqn in North Africa to fly the Spitfire VC. On 7 April Mackie shot down two Ju 87s and damaged two more near Medjez el Bab, in Tunisia. It was the start of an impressive career as a desert fighter pilot, and by the end of the year his tally had climbed to 18 enemy aircraft destroyed, probably destroyed or shared – most of his victories were over Bf 109s, although he also downed Ju 87s (three in one day), Fw 190s, a Do 217 and a pair of Italian Macchi C.202s.

Later, Mackie took command of No. 92 Sqn, flying Spitfire VIIIs over the Italian front. Here, he accounted for four more Bf 109s and an Fw 190, and by 2 February his score stood at 16. Subsequently returning to Britain, Mackie took a conversion course onto the Tempest at No. 83 Group Support Unit at Thorney Island, in west Sussex. He needed little convincing that in the Tempest V there was a fighter that was as good as the Spitfire. 'For the class of work that was in progress on the Continent,' Mackie recalled, 'and from what I could see of the Tempest, it had more to offer – greater firepower, greatly increased range and higher speed, particularly low down. It was particularly good in the dive and a very stable platform from which to fire.'

In December 1944 Mackie was posted to No. 274 Sqn at B.80 Volkel as a supernumerary squadron leader – a common practice for prospective COs faced with a new type and/or theatre – in order to gain some experience before taking command of their designated unit. The following month he took charge of No. 80 Sqn, co-located at B.80 Volkel. With these two squadrons Mackie would claim 11 enemy aircraft destroyed or damaged in the air or on the ground while flying the Tempest V. Mackie finished the war as Wing Commander Ops (previously known as Wing Commander Flying and colloquially as Wing Leader) No. 122 Wing.

Wg Cdr Evan Mackie scored 20 and three shared aerial victories, making him the RNZAF's leading ace. Returning to civilian life immediately post-war, he died on 28 April 1986.

Sqn Ldr Evan Dall 'Rosie' Mackie, seen here at B.80 Volkel in January 1945 when CO of No. 80 Sqn. (CT Collection)

HANS DORTENMANN

The most successful Fw 190D-9 pilot in terms of aerial victories was Hans Dortenmann, who claimed 18 kills while flying the type. His operational career reflects that of many Luftwaffe pilots on the Western Front in the final 12 months of the war.

Dortenmann was born on 11 December 1921 in Weingarten, in Baden-Württemberg. He commenced military service in the army as an infantryman, before transferring to the Luftwaffe in April 1941. His enthusiasm for hunting, a sport that was a tradition in his family, may have fuelled his ambition to become a fighter pilot to some extent, and following completion of flying training, he was assigned to 2./JG 54 on the Eastern Front in 1942, with whom he flew Fw 190As. However, having returned to the west for a period, Dortenmann suffered injuries as a result of a crash following a high-altitude flight over France on 9 April 1943. After four weeks in a military hospital he returned to active duty, and on 6 February 1944, while flying as wingman to future Knight's Cross-holder, and 86-victory ace, Unteroffizier Ulrich 'Seppl' Wöhnert, he scored his first victory when he collided with or possibly rammed a Soviet La-5 fighter. Despite damage to his Focke-Wulf's left wing, Dortenmann was able to return to Orscha-Süd airfield, where he carried out a successful belly-landing.

On 10 June 1944, as part of the new Luftwaffe policy to increase the strength of its *Jagdgruppen* to four *Staffeln* each, 2./JG 54 was removed from its parent *Gruppe* and transferred to III./JG 54 at Villacoublay, in north-central France, to where that *Gruppe* had been sent to combat the Allied invasion forces. By the time Dortenmann returned to France he had accumulated 14 confirmed kills, including four Il-2s, and on 20 June he was appointed *Kapitän* of 2. *Staffel*, which was redesignated 12./JG 54 on 10 August. Just four days after Dortenmann's appointment, however, he was forced to bail out of his badly shot up Fw 190 near Paris.

Although operations over France post-D-Day proved deadly and draining, Dortenmann was able to claim six enemy aircraft destroyed – a P-47, a P-51, two Spitfires and two P-38s.

Following III./JG 54's re-equipping with the Fw 190D-9, Dortenmann moved with 12./JG 54 to Achmer, from where he led airfield protection missions for the Me 262 jets of *Kommando Nowotny*. On Christmas Day 1944, III./JG 54 was placed under the tactical control of I./JG 26 for Operation *Bodenplatte*, the New Year's Day attack on Allied tactical airfields in France, Belgium and the Netherlands. Dortenmann

claimed a Spitfire on 29 December, but would not score again until 13 February, when he shot down a P-47 of the USAAF's 36th FG. When 12./JG 54 was disbanded on 19 February 1945, Dortenmann took command of 11./JG 54, which was subsequently redesignated 14./JG 26. Just over a month later he took command of 3./JG 26. This period saw him fly intensive ground attack operations, during which he destroyed several enemy vehicles and a flak battery position.

Hans Dortenmann was awarded the Knight's Cross on 20 April 1945, having achieved 35 victories, including claims for four Tempests. He carved for himself a reputation as an audacious fighter pilot, often choosing to close in to attack his opponents from very close range. He was also known to be combative with his superiors while looking after the interests of those who served under him. Dortenmann flew his last combat mission on 27 April, shooting down a Soviet Yak-3 over Berlin during the course of the sortie. His final victory tally was 38, of which 22 were over the Western Front and the rest in the East. Hans Dortenmann died on 1 April 1973.

The last *Staffelkapitän* of 3./JG 26, Oberleutnant Hans Dortenmann poses with his Knight's Cross, which he received on 20 April 1945. (EN-Archive)

COMBAT

A pristine Fieseler-built Fw 190D-9 of II./JG 26, probably recently delivered and purportedly photographed at Reinsehlen, although the *Gruppe* had left that base by mid-August 1944 and it did not receive its first D-9s until December of that year. The aircraft is fitted with a 300-litre drop tank and has a heavily mottled camouflage scheme. (EN-Archive)

For much of December 1944, the weather over the Western Front had precluded any significant operations by either the Luftwaffe or Allied air forces. Aircraft sat grounded on airfields shrouded in fog. The last German offensive in the West had opened on 16 December. Under the codename *'Die Wacht am Rhein'* ('The Watch on the Rhine'), Hitler wanted to drive an armoured wedge between the Allies by thrusting through the forests and hill country of the Ardennes to retake Antwerp. He also hoped that he could trap the American armies around Aachen, thus eliminating the threat posed to the Ruhr.

Fw 190D-9 Wk-Nr. 500342 of II./JG 26 has its engine run up at Reinsehlen in November 1944, the fighter being finished in a typical late-war style camouflage scheme. The *Gruppe* was undergoing conversion to the 'Dora' when this photograph was taken. The white '9' on the aircraft's rudder was not a tactical code but rather a temporary number used for ferry or delivery flights. (EN-Archive)

Finally, however, on the 23rd, the fog lifted and Allied air superiority was quickly re-established. The rail system upon which the Germans were so dependent for supplies was attacked by RAF and USAAF bombers, resulting in the Wehrmacht's Panzers being slowly starved of fuel. Simultaneously, fighter-bombers of the USAAF's Ninth Air Force began a systematic campaign in support of Allied ground forces. Hampered by Allied air power, weather and terrain, lacking fuel and meeting firm opposition, the German assault, still far short of Antwerp, faltered and stopped.

Since the improvement in the weather, the Tempest squadrons of 2nd TAF had been highly active undertaking their primary role of armed reconnaissance from their airfields in Belgium and the Netherlands. Their speed, firepower, range and all-round vision made them well-suited to such missions, and they also flew fighter sweeps and patrols. Ahead of any mission, briefings were carried out by the formation or unit leader in the Wing briefing room. Here, pilots would receive the latest information on enemy positions, movements and the location of friendly forces. Flak maps were studied, routes and heights set and R/T channels, diversionary landing grounds and safe areas confirmed – the latter were vital in the event of a pilot being forced down in enemy territory. An emphasis was also placed on accurate timekeeping throughout the course of the mission.

If an armed reconnaissance was planned, the area to be searched was discussed in detail, and if on the same mission a specific target was to be attacked, instructions were given on recognition, direction, method of attack and breakaway. With fighter sweeps, the emphasis was on aircraft call-signs, routes, heights and the position of the sun. In the case of patrols, the key factors were position of the sun, heights, ground control and speeds.

No. 3 Sqn opened the account on Christmas Eve as eight of its Tempests patrolled a line on an armed reconnaissance from Malmedy, in the Ardennes, to Jülich, in North Rhine-Westphalia. The RAF fighters ran into a formation of Bf 109s at 1240 hrs, and one of these was claimed shot down. Flg Off Rod Dryland (who had claimed 17 and 2 shared V1s destroyed during the summer) reported that he had downed an Fw 190D-9, only for his fighter to be hit by flak. Force-landing in enemy territory,

Dryland returned to Allied lines on foot two days later. However, there were no losses reported by III./JG 54 that day, and while all three *Gruppen* of JG 26 lost D-9s on 24 December, they were attributed to American fighters, friendly fire and engine trouble.

On Christmas Day a Tempest flown by Plt Off Reg Verran of No. 80 Sqn encountered an Ar 234B of the *Einsatzstaffel* of III./KG 76 and attempted to shoot it down. Verran (who ran out of ammunition during the engagement) and Wg Cdr John Wray, Wing Leader of No. 122 Wing, were both credited with a 'damaged' following this inconclusive clash. The Arado subsequently crash-landed at Teuge, in Holland, its pilot – who misidentified his attackers as Thunderbolts – escaping unhurt from the wreckage of his aircraft.

As mentioned in the previous chapter, the first, dramatic, test between the Tempest and the 'Dora' took place on 27 December in clear skies when eight aircraft from No. 486 Sqn on an armed reconnaissance to the Paderborn area encountered the 60 or so D-9s from III./JG 54 on a large-scale airfield protection flight for Ar 234s. The Tempests were flying in two 'finger-four' sections of four aircraft, while the D-9s were in a staggered formation at between 6,500–10,000ft, led by the *Stabsschwarm*. To the right and left of the *Stab* were, 9., 11. and 12. *Staffeln*, while flying top cover was 10. *Staffel* led by Leutnant Peter Crump, a 24-victory ace – all of his kills had been claimed in the West while flying with II./JG 26, and included Spitfires, Mustangs, P-47s and a Mosquito.

The two units met over the Münster area. On being alerted to the presence of the Tempests by ground control, the *Gruppenkommandeur*, Hauptmann Robert 'Bazzi' Weiss, a Knight's Cross-holder whose personal victory tally now stood at 122, ordered the large German formation to alter course from the southwest to the northeast. This split the lower *Staffeln* from Crump's *Staffel* and isolated it. Now highly vulnerable to attack, the pilots' position was made even worse when, as Crump ordered them to reverse, they lost contact, dispersed and lagged behind the rest of the *Gruppe*.

Leading the Tempest group was Sqn Ldr Keith Taylor-Cannon from Oamaru in New Zealand, who was known to his comrades as 'Hyphen' and who had a V1, shares in the destruction of an Me 262 and a Ju 188 to his name. 'We were flying at 10,000ft and sighted the Huns in two gaggles at "12 o'clock" to us,' he later reported, 'one formation of 15 109s and 190s at 9,000ft, with top cover of 20+ 109s and 190s at approximately 14,000ft.'

Taylor-Cannon led Red Section down into the enemy aircraft as Green Section climbed to engage 10./JG 54. The Tempests then pulled up in line astern and slightly below the lower-flying *Staffel* of D-9s. 'After breaking, I got on the tail of a Fw 190 and opened fire at 200 yards range,'

Clad in flying gear, Oberleutnant Hans Dortenmann (centre), *Staffelkapitän* of 12./JG 54, and four fellow pilots from 11. and 12. *Staffeln* trudge through the snow at Varrelbusch in early February 1945. (John Weal Collection)

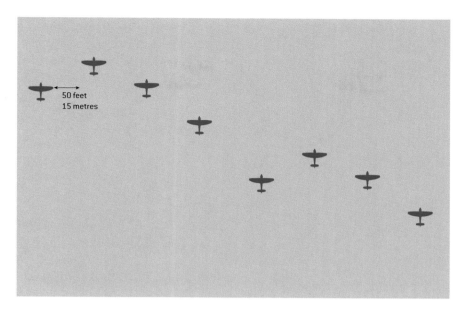

50 feet
15 metres

Following their arrival in northwest Europe in September 1944, Tempest V squadrons usually adopted eight- or sixteen-aircraft formations for flying out on sweeps, patrols and armed reconnaissance, comprised of two or four sections of four aircraft in a stepped line astern formation.

According to an immediate post-war report prepared by the Central Fighter Establishment (CFE) entitled 'Air Fighting Tactics used by Tempest Fighter Squadrons of 2nd TAF', for ascent, flight formation in cloudy weather was generally made with sections closed into close 'finger-four' formation, opening out into battle formation once in the clear, usually at 8,000–9,000ft. Fighter sweeps were usually carried out at 12,000–15,000ft, deploying a 'finger-four' type formation, with squadrons and sections stepped up away from the sun. This was also the standard tactic adopted to engage enemy formations.

In the 'finger-four', a section of four Tempests, each pair of aircraft spaced approximately 50ft apart, with the distance between each pair being some 200 yards, would fly roughly line abreast, with the distance between each section being approximately 400 yards. According to the CFE report, 'The importance of pilots keeping well up in line abreast so as to make full use of mutual cover could never be over-emphasised. A straggler was a menace to himself and his section.'

recounted Taylor-Cannon. 'I observed strikes, and as I pulled up sharply to avoid it, I saw the Fw 190 blow up in mid-air. A general dogfight ensued.'

Two pilots in Red Section, Plt Offs Sid J. Short and Keith A. Smith (also a V1 ace), each claimed an Fw 190 destroyed, the latter reporting:

I got into line astern, slightly above an Fw 190 and opened fire with a short burst from about 400 yards using half-a-ring of deflection. I closed the range, and when within 200 yards fired a short burst and another at very close range of 20 yards using a full ring of deflection. The Fw 190 blew up – I could not avoid the explosion but broke to starboard as I flew through it.

Short noted in his Combat Report:

I selected an Fw 190 and commenced firing from about 200 yards range in line astern, allowing five degrees of deflection. I held my fire for about two seconds and saw large puffs of grey-coloured smoke coming from beneath the fuselage. By this time I had an Me 109 [sic] on my tail firing at me so was forced to break to port and spun off. I did not see what happened to the Fw 190, but Red 4 – Flg Off Smith – saw it catch fire and the pilot bail out. After spinning off I recovered the spin and regained my section.

Meanwhile, Green Section had engaged Crump's *Staffel*. Flt Lt E. W. Tanner described how he:

. . . closed in behind a straggler of the enemy formation and identified it as an Fw 190 with a long-range tank. I fired a short burst from 200 yards range, allowing slight deflection and about five degrees off line astern but observed no strikes. Green 4 [Flg Off Smith] passed me very closely and I saw him open fire at the same aircraft from about 50 yards range. I saw the Fw 190 blow up in mid-air.

The Hun formation had broken so I climbed up through it and saw a long-nosed 190 flying across my nose at about 60 degrees and about 200 yards range. I opened fire, allowing 2½ rings of deflection and saw strikes on the tail unit, large pieces of which fell off. I saw the 190 roll over on its back and dive steeply to earth. Flg Offs Stafford and Danzey saw it going down vertically without its tail unit and pieces coming away from the fuselage. I milled around with the Section and then pulled up above the main gaggle. I spotted a 109 [sic] on the tail of a Tempest, so I dived on the 109 and opened fire at

Kiwi Plt Off Keith A. Smith (far left), flying a Tempest V of No. 486 Sqn, claimed an Fw 190D-9 of III./JG 54 shot down on 27 December 1944 during combat over the Münster area. Smith, who was also credited with eight V1s and an Me 262 destroyed, is seen here with fellow New Zealander, and ace, Flt Lt C. J. 'Jimmy' Sheddan (centre). (CT Collection)

about 400 yards, holding the burst until 150 yards. I saw strikes along the cockpit and saw the nose of the 109 go down as if the stick had gone violently forward. I was being engaged by about four other enemy aircraft so could not follow the 109 down, but Green 4 [Flg Off Smith] saw it tumbling down end over end.

The Tempest pilots had gone about their work quickly and efficiently, downing three Fw 190D-9s flown by Oberleutnant Paul Breger, Feldwebel Karl Dähn and Feldwebel Arnfried Köhler, all from 10./JG 54. Köhler came down by parachute with second-degree burns on his face and shrapnel in his foot. Breger suffered particular misfortune. Peter Crump had managed to turn tightly to position himself onto the tail of a Tempest that was itself pursuing another D-9 in his *Schwarm*. The RAF fighter was being flown by V1 ace Flg Off Bevan Hall of Green Section, who had come to the assistance of Flg Off Jack Stafford. According to Stafford, 'a 109 [sic] jumped on my tail and stayed there shooting, although without hitting me.'

Crump registered strikes on Flg Off Hall's Tempest, forcing him to bail out of his stricken machine as it fell away in a vertical dive. Moments later, the spiralling Tempest careered into Paul Breger's parachute as he floated down, having bailed out following Green Section's attack. The fighter crashed into the ground on the road between Handorf and Dorbaum, exploding on impact. Breger plummeted to earth with his parachute in flames and Hall was later found dead as well.

As the dogfight raged and drifted over Münster-Handorf airfield, Crump observed the D-9 of Unteroffizier Max Mittelstädt of 10. *Staffel* crash-land with its Jumo 213 on fire. As Mittelstädt, a former flight instructor from JG 103, attempted to land his aircraft, oil sprayed across his windscreen. He opened his canopy and tried to peer out, only to be splashed in the face with more hot oil. Mittelstädt, who lost consciousness as he crash-landed at the end of his very first combat sortie, was pulled from the wreckage of his now-wingless D-9 by another pilot.

From 12./JG 54, Feldwebel Walfried Huth crashed and was killed at Telgte and Unteroffizier Kurt Hein's D-9 was damaged. One German pilot wrote in his diary following the encounter, 'I just escaped from a wild dogfight with my skin. Our formation disintegrated completely, no trace of an "air battle", just wild confusion'. Another mentioned in a letter home, 'I must praise my machine.' The net result was that No. 486 Sqn had shot down five Fw 190D-9s and damaged another for the loss of Flg Off Bevan Hall and his Tempest. The men of the mauled 10./JG 54 were so harrowed by their experience that 'Bazzi' Weiss decided to rest them for a few days.

However, two days later, on 29 December, it would be Weiss who would be killed when the *Stabsschwarm* and 11./JG 54 entered combat with Spitfires and Typhoons over the Münster-Rheine area. The D-9s had been ordered to patrol at an altitude not to exceed 10,000ft, which meant that they would be vulnerable to attack by fighter-bombers from 2nd TAF. Sure enough, Weiss's flight encountered Spitfire IXs of No. 331 'Norwegian' Sqn and, having inflicted fatal damage on one of them, his 'Dora', 'Black 10', was shot down and crashed near Lengerich. Weiss, who held the distinction of having been the fourth most successful Luftwaffe fighter pilot over the Invasion front, and with 121 victories to his name, was killed. He would be posthumously awarded the Oak Leaves to the Knight's Cross on 12 March 1945.

For the rest of III./JG 54, the day would prove catastrophic as a result of poor tactical control and direction from the ground. In running combat with Typhoons and Spitfires, the *Gruppe* had 13 pilots killed and two wounded, meaning that in just two days of air fighting, the unit had suffered the loss or wounding of a third of its personnel.

The D-9 *Gruppen* would take further punishment on the day that Generalmajor Peltz, commander of II. *Jagdkorps*, had decided that the best way in which to offer support to the armoured thrust in the Ardennes was to neutralise Allied tactical air power where it was at its most vulnerable – on the ground. By using the element of surprise, Peltz concluded that as an alternative to costly dogfights against numerically superior and skilled enemy fighter pilots over the front, such an attack would incur minimum casualties and consume less fuel. Originally intended to coincide with the launch of the ground offensive, the weather frustrated the plan and the operation, codenamed *Bodenplatte* ('Base Plate'), was deferred, despite the commencement of *Wacht am Rhein*.

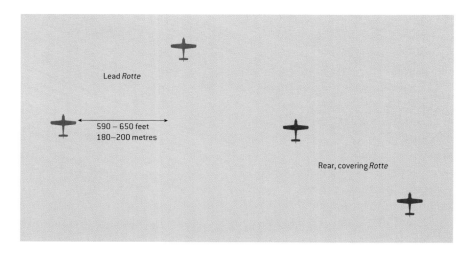

Lead *Rotte*

590 – 650 feet
180–200 metres

Rear, covering *Rotte*

The standard four-aircraft *Schwarm* fighter formation evolved from the earlier three-aircraft *Kette* used by pilots of the *Legion Condor* during the Spanish Civil War. A four-aircraft formation was found to offer greater in-flight cohesion and tactical flexibility. The *Schwarm* comprised two pairs – *Rotten* – in which one wingman, positioned behind, monitored and guarded the *Rottenführer's* (lead pilot's) course. The two *Rotten* flew in a loose line abreast formation, but with the rear *Rotte* echeloned back so that effectively the wingman concept extended by *Rotte* to the whole *Schwarm*, and resulted in a 'finger-four' formation, broadly resembling the fingers of an outstretched hand.

Radio communication also aided formation control and situational awareness. Generally, it was found that the best distance between aircraft was around 590–650ft. By scanning the sky inwards, blind spots below and behind could be covered. Quick turning was accomplished by the lead aircraft of the lead *Rotte* climbing and turning 90 degrees first, with his wingman following, followed by the rear *Rotte*, to result in a mirror/reverse line but with formation cohesion retained.

As the war progressed and different mission types ensued, so the optimum spacing between aircraft could change. For example, missions in Defence of the Reich would see tighter formation flying to bring together greater firepower against massed defensive firepower of enemy bomber formations. Larger formations would, in turn, be comprised of several *Schwarme*, with a lead *Schwarm* flying slightly ahead and other *Schwarme* positioned on either side, the one to the right staggered slightly further back.

The aircraft of Feldwebel Werner Hohenberg of the *Stabsschwarm* of I./JG 2 arouses the interest of two GIs as it lies wrecked in snowy countryside near the village of Dorff, near Stollberg, following its crash-landing during Operation *Bodenplatte* on 1 January 1945. Hohenberg's 'Dora' had been hit by fire from a US Army mobile flak battery while making a low-level pass over the airfield at A.92 St. Trond. The D-9 carries the chevron and bars of a *Stab* aircraft, as well as the yellow-white-yellow fuselage band markings of JG 2. (EN-Archive)

At the first suitable break in the weather – dawn on 1 January 1945 – German fighters from 33 *Gruppen* left their forward bases and roared in tight formation at low-level towards the Allied lines. Although complete surprise was achieved and moderate success gained at B.78 Eindhoven (where two Canadian Typhoon squadrons were virtually destroyed), B.58 Brussels-Melsbroek and B.61 St. Denis-Westrem, the attacks on B.70 Antwerp/Duerne, A.92 Le Culot and B.80 Volkel were nothing short of catastrophic.

The bulk of the D-9 force comprised I. and III./JG 2 and I. and II./JG 26, the latter *Geschwader* also being assigned III./JG 54. JG 2's attack on A.92 St. Trond was a total failure, with the *Geschwader* losing half of its force in the operation, while things were little better in the strikes on B.56 Brussels-Evere and B.60 Grimbergen by JG 26 and JG 54. II./JG 26 did operate according to schedule and it did find and attack its target at B.56 Brussels-Evere, claiming the destruction of 20 B-17s and B-24s, 24 twin-engined aircraft and 60 fighters – the Allies reported the loss of 45 aircraft on the ground here. Certainly, 15 Spitfires were destroyed or damaged, as well as several Ansons, Austers and Dakotas, including those belonging to the commander of 2nd TAF! JG 26 in turn had no fewer than 22 Fw 190D-9s destroyed or damaged during *Bodenplatte*, mostly by 'friendly' flak.

As February 1945 came around, RAF and USAAF fighters virtually ruled the skies over Germany, and even though the Luftwaffe could still – sporadically – hit back, for the Allies the air war was fast becoming a game of 'cat and mouse'. But it was still a tough, deadly game.

In the pre-dawn hours of 28 February, the commanders of two units briefed their pilots. At Plantlünne, in northern Germany, one of the Luftwaffe's most stellar aces, Hauptmann Walter Krupinski, holder of the Knight's Cross with Oak Leaves and the claimant of 195 victories since 1941, addressed the pilots of III./JG 26 – a *Gruppe* he had led since late September 1944. For most of the month the *Gruppe* had been

ENGAGING THE ENEMY

The pilot of an Fw 190D-9 banks his aircraft as he tries to bring a Tempest V into the reflector sight of his 'Revi' (Reflexvisier) 16B during a climbing chase. The Tempest could not compete with the 'Dora' in the climb, but could out-dive it and compared favourably with the Focke-Wulf in a turn. The Revi 16B is seen mounted on the top of the instrument panel. This sight required the pilot to estimate the angle of deflection to the target according to combat conditions. However, in reality, this could only be done with any degree of accuracy when engaging at short range and/or when attacking from a central position with minimum deflection.

When not required, the sight could be collapsed or folded away to one side. The Revi 16B incorporated a sun visor, night vision filter, light bulb and dimmer switch.

The pilot's left hand grips the throttle lever, while his right pulls on the control column, with his thumb on the firing button for the 20mm MG 151/20E wing-mounted cannon. The Fw 190D-9 featured one of the earliest examples of a cockpit designed with relative comfort and ergonomics in mind, so that all main levers and controls such as the starter switch, undercarriage manual lowering handle, oxygen flow valve and communications and IFF controls were in easy reach.

training up on its new D-9s, this task being made difficult since at Plantlünne the end of the airfield routinely 'disappeared' in freezing rain. A number of aircraft had been lost or damaged as a result. Nevertheless, orders were received instructing the unit to fly a mission in *Geschwader* strength against enemy fighter-bombers supporting the American advance on Mönchen-Gladbach. This would be III./JG 26's first mission with its 'Doras', and Krupinski led the entire *Gruppe* up from Plantlünne at around 0730 hrs.

Meanwhile, at B.80 Volkel, Sqn Ldr David Fairbanks of No. 274 Sqn briefed five of his pilots for an early morning armed reconnaissance to Hamm, Münster and Osnabrück. An American who had joined the Royal Canadian Air Force (RCAF) in 1941, serving initially in Nos. 501 and 3 Sqns, Fairbanks had been described by No. 274 Sqn's diarist as the 'terror of Rheine' on account of the fact that he regularly visited that Luftwaffe jet base at some risk, but with some success. Fairbanks had 11.5 victories to his name, which included a V1 flying bomb, Bf 109s, Fw 190s (two of which were D-9s from III./JG 54 claimed near Rheine on 22 February) and an Ar 234.

The six Tempests, formed into two sections, took off at 0718 hrs and headed east towards Germany. Some nine miles east of Osnabrück at 5,500ft, they spotted III./JG 26's Fw 190D-9s flying south about 500ft above them – the latter were identified as '40+ Fw 190s and Me 109s'. Fairbanks instructed his pilots to release their drop tanks and make a head-on attack. Within moments they turned into the 'Doras' and joined them in a swirling air battle, the greatly outnumbered Tempest pilots finding it impossible to keep formation as the D-9s swept in, forcing them to literally fly and fight for their lives. Three of the *'langnasen'* attempted to turn in line astern with the Tempest flown by Canadian Flg Off Fred Mossing:

In doing so, I was able to fire deflection shots at the No. 3. I made about five passes, firing from one- to two-second bursts at angles from 40 degrees down to 5 degrees, and closing from 400 yards to 100 yards. I saw strikes on the fuselage in one attack, and the enemy aircraft streamed black smoke but went into cloud. I pulled up but was unable to see the Hun.

D-9s also 'jumped' the Tempest of Flt Sgt A. E. 'Ben' Gunn, who put up a fight:

I attacked a Fw 190 from 400 yards line astern and saw strikes on the fuselage. The enemy aircraft climbed into clouds pouring smoke so I followed and fired again from 150 yards astern in light cloud. He broke straight down to port and I lost him. I came out of cloud and fired at another Fw 190 from 400 yards with two rings of deflection and saw strikes on its tail. I attacked a third Fw 190 from 400 yards range, 60 degrees off, and observed strikes in the port wing. I was then hit badly in the port wing but managed to climb back into cloud and make for base.

A 'black man' (the name given to all Luftwaffe groundcrew due to the colour of their overalls) watches as Fw 190D-9s of 7./JG 26 taxi out from their forested dispersal at Nordhorn-Klausheide in February 1945. Timber planks have been thrown down haphazardly to aid traction in the muddy conditions. (EN-Archive)

Flt Sgt A. C. Inglis, flying in Blue section as No. 2, endeavoured to stay behind his No. 1 as combat commenced. The two Tempests turned tightly to port, with Inglis latching on to the tail of two 'Doras' that were chasing his leader. Inglis fired a two-second burst at 200 yards and watched as one of the Focke-Wulfs flicked onto its back. He fired again and saw strikes hit the second German fighter in the port wing, at which point he was forced to wrestle with the controls of his Tempest to prevent it flicking into a spin as his port drop tank refused to jettison. Inglis then had his guns jam with 70 rounds remaining in each. 'I broke through three Fw 190s that were attacking me,' Inglis reported, 'went into cloud and headed for base.'

Meanwhile, Fairbanks found himself in the thick of it. 'I don't remember any return fire from the enemy aircraft. I think they were just as surprised as we were,' he later recalled. Fairbanks initially chased a Focke-Wulf until it escaped, after which he dropped down into some cloud. As he emerged, he spotted another D-9, but by now he was without his wingman:

I closed the range on this aircraft and before I was ready to fire I noticed some tracers coming my way. I was near the ground and thought it was flak tracer. A few more tracers went by me and I was ready to fire at the enemy aircraft. I fired and hit the '190, which burst into flames. The next instant I was hit hard.

It was not ground tracer I had seen but shells from the aircraft behind that hit me. I can remember seeing wing ribs and torn skin on the left and right upper wing surfaces, and I was having difficulty keeping the aircraft level. The engine was missing and puffs of glycol were shooting by. No doubt my rad[iator] had been punctured. I held the stick hard over right to keep level and applied right rudder. With the controls in these positions I knew I wasn't going home. I decided it was time to bail out.

Holding the controls with my right hand, I tried to jettison the canopy with my left, but it wouldn't budge. I tried several times but didn't have enough strength in my left hand alone. I let go of the controls and pulled the jettison handle with both hands and away she went. I can only remember that the canopy was gone and that I leaned my head to the left into the slipstream. The next thing I remember I was on the ground.

'Black men' work on an Fw 190D-9 of 3./JG 26 'hidden' in its wooded dispersal at Fürstenau in February 1945. The aircraft is carrying a 170-litre drop tank on its centreline rack, behind which can be seen the aerial for the FuG 16ZY VHF transceiver. (EN-Archive)

Wg Cdr Evan Dall Mackie, CO of No. 80 Sqn, breaks away from other Tempest Vs in NV700/W2-A during air-to-air filming on 21 March 1945. He had been at the controls of this aircraft when he emerged victorious from a testing engagement with an Fw 190D-9 that was almost certainly flown by Unteroffizier Otto Salewski of 10./JG 26 two weeks earlier on 7 March. (CT Collection)

The air filled with the noise of its Napier Sabre engine, NV93?/SA-C rolls out at B.80 Volkel in March 1945. This aircraft flew with No. 486 Sqn for just 15 days before suffering damage. After being repaired it was re-assigned to No. 3 Sqn, with whom it became JF-J. (CT Collection)

Fairbanks, whose last radio call to his squadronmates had been 'Five on my tail', was made a PoW (he had to be rescued by a German flak officer from an angry crowd of civilians), while fellow Tempest pilot Flg Off J. B. Spence was listed as missing – he too was captured. Claims for Tempests were lodged by Oberleutnant Theobald Kraus, the leader of 10./JG 26, and by Unteroffizier Karl-Georg Genth of 12. *Staffel*. On the German side, three D-9s crashed-landed during the battle, but only Unteroffizier Franz Schmidt of 9./JG 26 died as a result of injuries sustained. Fairbanks subsequently claimed an Fw 190D destroyed after he was released post-war, although it was never formally recorded by the RAF. Gunn was credited with three Fw 190s damaged, and Mossing and Inglis also claimed a single Focke-Wulf damaged apiece.

A week later, another encounter served to indicate how balanced the Tempest V and Fw 190D-9 were when flown by experienced pilots, and how demanding and draining air combat could be. At 1400 hrs on the afternoon of 7 March 1945, Tempests from Nos. 3 and 56 Sqns took off on patrols of the Rheine area. They were followed 31 minutes later by a Wing formation of Tempests drawn from Nos. 80, 274 and 486 Sqns led by Sqn Ldr Evan Mackie, CO of No. 80 Sqn. These squadrons were flying a sweep to the Nienburg-Hannover-Hamm areas.

At Plantlünne, orders were received from *Luftwaffenkommando West* for III./JG 26 to carry out a full-strength *freie Jagd* ('free patrol') to Enschede. Because of the unavailability of more senior formation leaders, the mission was to be led by Oberfeldwebel Willi Zester of 9. *Staffel*, who, although an experienced pilot, had never previously led a formation. Eventually, after waiting at cockpit readiness for some

On 7 March 1945, Sqn Ldr Evan
Mackie of No. 80 Sqn engaged an
Fw 190D-9 in a fierce dogfight
near Enschede. The latter aircraft
was probably Wk-Nr. 400247
'Black 4', flown by Unteroffizier
Otto Salewski of 10./JG 26. While
climbing up to 8,000ft, Mackie,
who was in Tempest NV700/W2-A,
had initially spotted the vapour
trails of six to eight Focke-Wulfs
above him at about 15,000ft.
Continuing to climb through
patchy cloud, he and his
squadron intercepted the 'Doras'
at around 13,000ft as they were
diving down to attack other
Tempests. Mackie singled out
Salewski, chasing him vertically
down to 3,000ft. For the next five
minutes the two fighters duelled
over the flat, open countryside
between Plantlünne and Rheine
until Mackie, aided by the arrival
of two more Tempests from
No. 274 Sqn, fired a
one-and-a-half-second burst,
with 30 degrees of deflection,
from approximately 200 yards.
Flames tailed back from the
Focke-Wulf's cockpit and it
crashed 'in a mushroom of smoke
and flame' north of Rheine near
the village of Schüttorf. Salewski
perished.

time, 17 Fw 190D-9s took off from Plantlünne, climbing to 9,850ft and flying directly to Enschede. Here, they found the skies to be active with Spitfires and Typhoons. Turning back east towards Rheine, the Focke-Wulfs were on a 'collision course' with the Tempests of Nos. 80, 274 and 486 Sqns, whose pilots spotted the Luftwaffe formation first at 13,000ft at 1545 hrs north of the town. They quickly engaged the German fighters, although III./JG 26 had by then already committed to attacking another formation of Tempests (probably from Nos. 3 and 56 Sqns). As Mackie, flying with No. 80 Sqn, reported:

> Climbing through cloud at about 8,000ft, I saw about six or eight aircraft making vapour trails at approximately 15,000ft. So climbing up we eventually made contact at about 13,000ft as the enemy aircraft were diving down on other Tempests. I picked out a long-nosed Fw 190 which, after several manoeuvres dived vertically down to 3,000ft, just below a five-tenths layer of cumulus cloud. I then found myself alone with this 190, over open country, so we proceeded to have a good, uninterrupted dogfight.

Mackie's opponent was almost certainly Unteroffizier Otto Salewski of 10./JG 26 who had joined the *Geschwader* from pilot training in November 1943. Salewski had been wounded on 6 February 1944 when his Bf 109G-6 had been attacked by a P-47 over Paris, and he was forced to bail out of his Messerschmitt on 23 March while flying with 12. *Staffel* after he was attacked by an escort fighter during a USAAF bombing raid. Despite suffering severe injuries on landing, Salewski eventually returned to operational service and, by the standards of Reich defence missions, he was now a 'veteran'.

Mackie continued:

> For over five minutes I tried to position myself for a reasonable shot at him, but he proved to be a very clueful opponent. We were both leaving almost continuous wingtip trails. I found that with full revs and boost, I could gain slowly on him in about three complete turns, but when almost ready to open fire at him, he would throttle back suddenly and turn sharply, causing me to overshoot. These tactics were to some extent successful, and he actually took one wild shot at me on one occasion, but the deflection was full and he must have been almost stalled at the time, so I was not unduly worried. After each of these overshoots, I found myself back where I started, and so another vicious turning circle developed. Once or twice he attempted to dive away on the deck, climbing up again when I began gaining on him, and he even went up into cloud, which was not sufficient cover for him.

Mackie was eventually relieved by the arrival of two Tempests from No. 274 Sqn, which served to distract the German pilot. He was able to fire a 1.5-second burst with 30 degrees deflection from approximately 200 yards. Fire broke out in the D-9's cockpit, which then engulfed the aircraft. It crashed in a mushroom of smoke and flame north of Rheine. Mackie returned to B.80 Volkel drenched in sweat from what he considered to be the hardest encounter of his career. After the war, he commented that, 'The Tempest could not compete with the Hun in a climb, but could out-dive them with ease and compared favourably in the turn.'

JG 26 lost two pilots killed that day, namely Salewski and the inexperienced Leutnant Heinz-Wilhelm Bartels of 11. *Staffel*. Two others were wounded.

For much of March, Tempest sorties were curtailed and ground attack operations were stopped. Missions into enemy territory had to be undertaken with at least 16 aircraft and when, later in the month, Tempests and D-9s met again in the air, the results were not only confusing but marred by overclaiming on both sides.

On the cloudless day of 22 March, 12 Fw 190D-9s of II./JG 26 under Hauptmann Paul Schauder had been ordered up from Nordhorn during the mid-afternoon to intercept B-26 Marauder tactical bombers from the Ninth Air Force. However, before they managed to engage the USAAF aircraft, they were bounced near Lingen by Tempests from Nos. 56 and 80 Sqns on a fighter sweep over Rheine and the Minden-Dummer See areas. Flt Lts J. T. Hodges and G. B. Milne, Flg Off V. L. Turner and Sgt P. C. Brown of No. 56 Sqn and Flt Lt R. C. Cooper and Flg Off G. A. Bush of No. 80 Sqn claimed to have shot down six 'Doras', with two more damaged. In reality, 5./JG 26 reported the loss of Unteroffizier Edwin Kalbus and 6. *Staffel* had Unteroffizier Günter Issleib, Obergefreiter Otto Putschenjack and Leutnant Willi Wiese shot down, with Unteroffizier Günther Warthemann being wounded. The Germans in turn claimed two RAF fighters downed when, in fact, all the Tempests returned to base.

25 March would also prove to be a hard day for the D-9 units. The *Gruppenkommandeur* of I./JG 2, Hauptmann Franz Hrdlicka, was shot down in his fighter near Betzenrod, in Hessen. A seasoned unit commander with experience gained in some 500 missions over the Eastern and Italian fronts, Hrdlicka was a holder

Marked with a command pennant just forward of the cockpit, EJ886/5R-N was the usual mount of South African Sqn Ldr A. W. 'Bill' Bower, CO of No. 33 Sqn. He claimed one of the unit's first kills with it (a Bf 109 of JG 27) on 25 February 1945 and was credited with sharing in the destruction of an Fw 190D-9 (from I./JG 26) on 26 March 1945, again while flying EJ886. No. 33 Sqn had taken on its first Tempest Vs at Predannack, in Cornwall, in December 1944, the aircraft replacing Spitfire IXs. It joined No. 135 Wing at B.77 Gilze-Rijen in February 1945. (CT Collection)

A veteran of 260 missions and holder of the Knight's Cross, Oberleutnant Karl-Wilhelm Hofmann served exclusively with JG 26 during his two-and-a-half years in the frontline. He had just downed a Tempest V for his 44th victory (a tally that included six four-engined bombers) on 26 March 1945 when his 'Dora' was accidentally fired upon by a pilot from I. *Gruppe*. Hofmann bailed out, but at too low a height for his parachute to open. (Donald L. Caldwell Collection)

of the Knight's Cross (he would be posthumously awarded the Oak Leaves) with at least 44 victories to his name. That same day I./JG 26 suffered losses when Tempests of No. 222 Sqn bounced its D-9s as they formed up over their new base of Drope. Three Focke-Wulfs were quickly despatched, although two pilots managed to bail out. Fähnrich Heinrich Hermann, having just transferred to 1. *Staffel* that morning from 10./JG 26, was not so fortunate, being killed in action with the Tempests 12 miles southwest of Meppen.

For the Luftwaffe, the attrition in both aircraft and pilots was becoming critical. Despite eight Fw 190D-9s of I. and II./JG 26 launching an attack on Tempests of No. 33 Sqn during the afternoon of the 26th southeast of Münster, the RAF pilots managed to turn the tables and engage their assailants. Although WO C. A. Ligtenstein was forced to bail out of his Tempest after it was shot up by Oberleutnant Karl-Wilhelm Hofmann, the *Kapitän* of 5. *Staffel*, for his 44th victory, Sqn Ldr A. W. Bower and Flt Sgt C. B. Nisbet claimed an Fw 190D shot down between them and Flg Off R. H. Brown was credited with a second 'Dora' destroyed and a third damaged. In fact, the Tempests succeeded in shooting down all three, with Unteroffizier Gerhard Reichow of 1. *Staffel* and Oberfähnrich Wolfgang Franz of 3. *Staffel* being killed near Münster-Lengerich, while Leutnant Wilhelm Blickle, also of 3./JG 26, escaped with wounds.

It was an especially bitter day for II./JG 26, for shortly after having shot down WO Ligtenstein, Oberleutnant Hofmann was accidentally fired upon by a pilot from I. *Gruppe*. The *Staffelkapitän* bailed out, but at too low a height for his parachute to open. His body was eventually found on 2 April. Another Knight's Cross-holder had been lost.

Occasionally the Luftwaffe hit back. At 1105 hrs on 28 March, 12 D-9s from IV./JG 26, led by the redoubtable Oberleutnant Hans Dortenmann, took off for a patrol. After less than 30 minutes, having made it as far as Münster, the German formation spotted and bounced Tempests of No. 56 Sqn on a late morning armed reconnaissance. Sgt S. A. Sheppard failed to return from the Hannover-Osnabrück area and became Dortenmann's 31st victory when the German ace shot him down southwest of Münster.

Dortenmann struck again on 12 April. Leading 12 D-9s of I./JG 26 out from Stade in clear skies at 1230 hrs to attack targets across the Weser, the German formation quickly spotted eight Tempests passing beneath them. These were aircraft from No. 33 Sqn flying a sweep. The Focke-Wulf pilots dropped their tanks and dived

to attack. A wild, turning dogfight began north of Uelzen, with aircraft weaving from 2,600ft down to ground level. Aviators from JG 26 subsequently claimed five victories and one probable, although Leutnant Erich Asmus of the *Gruppenstab* was in turn killed.

Dortenmann lodged claims for two Tempests and Leutnant Waldemar Söffing one, while from No 33 Sqn, Capt E. D. Thompson of the South African Air Force and fellow countryman Flg Off D. J. ter Beek each claimed a 'Dora' shot down, with ter Beek damaging two more. However, Thompson's aircraft was so badly damaged that it was written off. Indeed, on this occasion the Tempests had come off worst. Despite the Germans over-claiming, Flt Sgt P. W. C. Watton and Sgt J. Staines were both shot down, the former surviving and evading capture and the latter being killed. Watton apparently also claimed one of the attackers shot down, probably Asmus.

The war in northwest Europe ground on for another three weeks, but by the end of April the *Jagdwaffe* was in a state of systematic disbandment and collapse. On 1 May, British forces continued their drive across northern Germany and advanced from the Elbe towards Berlin virtually unopposed. Adolf Hitler had just committed suicide and Hermann Göring was under house arrest in southern Germany for attempting to seize control of what remained of the Third Reich as a result of the *Führer*'s self-imposed incarceration. In the air, the *Jagdwaffe* continued its last, spasmodic but defiant defensive operations on both the Western and Eastern fronts. Allied air power was simply too strong a force, however, and within a week the war was over.

A formation of 16 Tempest Vs (the 16th aircraft is out of the shot), comprised of eight fighters each from Nos. 80 (nearest to the camera) and 486 Sqns (furthest), with each units' aircraft split into two sections of four in line astern. Such formations were usually only seen when squadrons were joining up immediately after take-off as pilots circled their airfield, prior to splitting up into 'finger-four' tactical formation and heading into enemy territory. (CT Collection)

STATISTICS AND ANALYSIS

In late 1944, the Tempest V and Fw 190D-9 represented the state-of-the-art in piston-engined fighter design in northwest Europe, these types being comparable to the Spitfire XIV, the P-51D and Bf 109K-4. Both aircraft were also the result of correction, alteration and refinement, the 'Dora' design taking the Fw 190A-8 fuselage and extending both it and the cowling in order to accommodate the Jumo 213 engine, while Hawker set out to improve the Tempest's high-altitude performance over the Typhoon by narrowing the wing.

Ultimately, the Tempest edged the D-9 in overall performance. The latter's wing loading was higher and the Tempest was able to out-turn the German fighter with relative ease. It was only in the rate of roll that the D-9 held the advantage.

In early December 1943, two test pilots from the USAAF Materiel Command's Flight Section visited the Hawker factory at Langley to assess the new Tempest V. Offering a neutral view, they noted that the cockpit was shorter than most American contemporary fighters, which placed the gunsight close to the pilot's eye, but that its positioning interfered with the instrument panel. Furthermore, some controls were cumbersome and confusing. On the ground, the Tempest was considered 'pleasant to handle', while during take-off there was an appreciable tendency for a right-hand swing, although the rudder was sufficient to hold the aircraft straight. In the air, the aircraft was found to handle 'pleasingly well' over the entire speed range, and manoeuvrability and vision were good. The Americans concluded that, 'The Tempest V should prove to be a very excellent fighter airplane. It is easy to fly and exhibits very desirable fighter characteristics, coupled with excellent performance.'

FAR LEFT
The last *Staffelkapitän* of
13./JG 26, Leutnant Peter Crump
claimed all 24 of his victories
(including seven four-engined
bombers) in the West. Initially
serving with JG 53 in 1940–41,
he transferred to JG 26 in June
1942 and remained with the
Jagdgeschwader through to war's
end. Shot down twice by
Thunderbolts during the course of
302 missions, Crump survived
the conflict. (Donald L. Caldwell
Collection)

LEFT
New Yorker Sqn Ldr David 'Foob'
Fairbanks had joined the RCAF in
1941 and served as an instructor
in Canada until being sent to
Britain in 1943. He subsequently
saw combat from the spring of
1944 in Spitfire VBs with
No. 501 Sqn, downing a
Bf 109 48 hours after the D-Day
landings. Transferring to
Tempest V-equipped No. 274 Sqn
in August of that year, Fairbanks
had downed two more Bf 109s
and a V1 by the time he joined
No. 3 Sqn in late December 1944.
Credited with a further
3.5 victories in January 1945, he
returned to No. 254 Sqn as its CO
on 8 February. Although
Fairbanks' period in charge would
last just 20 days, he would claim
seven kills – including four
Fw 190Ds – prior to being shot
down and captured on
28 February. (CT Collection)

Sqn Ldr Evan Mackie of No. 80 Sqn, who became one of the top-scorers in the Tempest, recorded that it 'seemed to have very few faults in my opinion. It could be thrown around the sky like a piece of paper, it was so manoeuvrable.'

By comparison, in 1946 Materiel Command test pilots flew a captured D-9, and concluded that 'the Fw 190D-9, although well armoured and equipped to carry heavy armament, appears to be much less desirable from a handling standpoint than other models of the Fw 190 using the BMW 14-cylinder radial engine. Any advantage that this aircraft may have in performance over other models of the Fw 190 is more than offset by its poor handling characteristics.'

German impressions of the D-9 are harder to come by. In assessing the Focke-Wulf, Leutnant Karl-Heinz Ossenkop, a pilot with 2./JG 26, recalled:

I was struck by the high quality of my new mount. The joints of aluminium sheeting and the riveting were very smooth, helping to reduce drag. Overall, we pilots of JG 26 were very pleased with these new machines. Yes, we were doubtful at first, but we became more confident and felt we were at least equal or, in some cases, even better [than the enemy in their latest fighter types], allowing us to win the battle in a Fw 190D-9.

Fellow D-9 pilot Hauptmann Roderich Cescotti, who commanded II./JG 301 at Stendal, Neustadt-Glewe and Leck, felt that the 'Dora' was a 'splendid machine' which suffered from few technical failures. In his view the greatest challenge was a lack of fuel in the Third Reich by early 1945.

In terms of production, of a total 1,399 Tempests built, 802 were Tempest Vs. In Germany, the actual number of Fw 190D-9s completed is not known, and considerable discrepancies exist in official figures. However, it seems that around 900 aircraft were

Fähnenjunker-Oberfeldwebel Heinz Marquardt (right) of 13./JG 51 surveys the damage done to his Fw 190D-9 when he accidentally ran into a drainage ditch at the start of a short transfer flight between fields to the north of Berlin on 30 April 1945. With no replacement available for that splintered VS 9 propeller, 'White 11' had to be blown up to prevent it falling into Soviet hands. Marquardt claimed 22 victories in the D-9 between 14 April and 1 May 1945 during a series of fierce engagements with Soviet fighters and ground attack aircraft. He was shot down on the latter date by a Spitfire XIV from No. 41 Sqn, although he survived the ordeal. Marquardt claimed 121 victories (all in the East) during 320 sorties. (John Weal Collection)

built (129 machines had been completed by Focke-Wulf, Weser and Fieseler to 1 November 1944).

Beyond speed, manoeuvrability and armament, it is the experience and skill of a pilot that turns a good aeroplane into a superlative one. The highest-scoring Tempest ace was Sqn Ldr David 'Foob' Fairbanks, credited with 11 victories on the type (he claimed an Fw 190D-9 as his 12th just prior to being shot down, but this remained unconfirmed) from a total score of 15. His counterpart in the D-9 was Oberleutnant Hans Dortenmann, who flew the 'Dora' with JG 54 and JG 26 and shot down 18 enemy aircraft in the *'Langnase'*. This tally made him the most successful pilot on the type by some margin.

Records are frustratingly scant on the individual scores achieved by Luftwaffe airmen flying the D-9, but those pilots believed to have claimed multiple kills include Oberleutnant Peter Crump of 10./JG 54 and 13./JG 26; Major Anton Hackl, the *Kommodore* of JG 11 whose *Stab* took delivery of the type from early 1945, followed by III. *Gruppe*; Fahnenjunker-Oberfeldwebel Heinz Marquardt of 13./JG 51; and Leutnant Waldemar Söffing of I./JG 26, whose last victory – his 34th – was over a Tempest on 29 April 1945 when he shot one down south of Lübeck while flying an escort for Fw 190F fighter-bombers of 12./SG 151. This may well have been the aircraft of WO A. Crowe of No. 3 Sqn, who came down north of Gresse unhurt. Söffing was recommended for the Knight's Cross.

However, what can be ascertained is that with the exception of Dortenmann, Marquardt and possibly Söffing, most other scorers on the D-9 would have claimed at the most four kills with the aircraft. By comparison, the Allied account on Tempests appears more impressive:

	Tempest Victories (excluding V1s)	Previous Successes	Unit(s)
Sqn Ldr D. C. Fairbanks RCAF	11 or 12 and 1 shared	+1	Nos. 3 and 274 Sqns
Wg Cdr W. E. Schrader RNZAF	9 and 1 shared	+2 and 1 shared	No. 486 Sqn
Flt Lt J. J. Payton	6	-	No. 56 Sqn
Wg Cdr E. D. Mackie RNZAF	5 and 1 shared	+16 and 1 shared	No. 80 Sqn and No. 122 Wing
Flg Off D. E. Ness RCAF	5 and 1 shared	-	No. 56 Sqn
Sqn Ldr C. J. Sheddan RNZAF	4 and 3 shared	-	No. 486 Sqn
Flt Lt P. H. Clostermann French	4	+7	Nos. 274, 56 and 3 Sqns
Flt Lt A. R. Evans RNZAF	4	-	No. 486 Sqn
Flt Lt J. W. Garland RCAF	4	-	Nos. 80 and 3 Sqns
Sqn Ldr A. R. Moore	4	-	No. 56 Sqn
Flg Off V. L. J. Turner RAAF	4	-	No. 56 Sqn

As can be seen, most high scorers on the Tempest were drawn from the Commonwealth, although David Fairbanks was actually an American serving in the RCAF. Indeed, the number of nationalities involved was impressive – New Zealanders from No. 486 Sqn, as well as pilots from the RCAF, Royal Australian Air Force, South African Air Force, the Netherlands, India, Norway, the USA and Greece.

The first three Tempest units were all Typhoon squadrons that had re-equipped with the new Hawker fighter. This was initially seen by Fighter Command as the most desired policy, but it would soon be abandoned when Typhoon squadrons were urgently required for service with 2nd TAF. Indeed, the next units to receive Tempests had all previously flown Spitfires. There seems to have been no great attempt to fill these units with aces or very experienced pilots, except when it came to flight commanders and squadron leaders (i.e., the likes of Evan Mackie and Warren Schrader). Quite a few pilots serving with Tempest squadrons had gained considerable instructor experience, but seen little in the way of frontline action. Expressing a keenness to get onto 'ops' before war's end, they routinely joined the Tempest squadrons at the same time as new pilots arriving from OTUs.

New Zealander Sqn Ldr Warren E. Schrader RNZAF found himself in the thick of the action with No. 486 Sqn from 10 April through to 1 May 1945, claiming nine and one shared aerial victories in the Tempest V. All of his victories were fighters, including five Fw 190s (some of which were D-9s). Schrader ended the war as CO of Meteor III-equipped No. 616 Sqn, claiming three strafing victories in the jet on 3 May. (CT Collection)

AFTERMATH

Refinement too late. The rare Fw 190D-13 Wk-Nr.836017 'Yellow 10', formerly of *Stab* JG 26 at Gilze-Rijen, after its flight to Flensburg. Here, having had USAAF markings applied (a white star can just be seen on the underside of each wing), it was flown at least twice by veteran aces from JG 51 in mock combat against a Tempest V. Seen to advantage here is the large paddle-bladed VS 9 propeller, and the fact that there was no provision for outboard wing guns. (EN-Archive)

Both the Tempest V and the Fw 190D-9 were amongst the few fighters to see service in World War II that had been designed after the outbreak of hostilities. Despite them being excellent all-round aircraft, by mid-1945 the sun was beginning to set on the era of piston-engined fighters as jet engine technology rapidly progressed.

Intriguingly, however, examples of each type would meet in the air after the cessation of hostilities. In 2009, aviation historian Jerry Crandall published an account of how 'Dora' Wk-Nr. 836017 'Yellow 10' had been assigned to JG 26 and became the aircraft of the *Geschwaderkommodore,* Major Franz Götz. At the end of the war, the aircraft ended up in Flensburg as the unit surrendered to British forces. While here, RAF disarmament and technical personnel were eager to discover more about the sleek-looking fighter, so they duly invited 73-victory ace Major Heinz Lange (former *Kommodore* of JG 51 and a Knight's Cross-holder), who was 'resident' at Flensburg and whose unit had also been equipped with the D-9, to take part in mock combat with a Tempest V.

The dogfight duly took place, with the Tempest flown by a Canadian pilot and with limited fuel in each machine. The aircraft seemed equal to each other in 'combat', and

Lange felt that the result of any dogfight was down to the individual skill of the pilots involved. The 'Dora' was flown for a second time on 25 June 1945 in another comparison flight against the Tempest, but on this occasion former *Kommandeur* of IV./JG 51, 178-victory ace Oberleutnant Günther Josten, was at the controls. It seems the Allies were sufficiently impressed with the performance of the Focke-Wulf to want to take examples back to Britain and the USA for further evaluation.

What Lange incorrectly assumed was that he had been flying a D-9. He had not. The aircraft used in mock combat against the Tempest had been a D-13. This was a revised D-model sub-variant built with an MG 151 engine-mounted cannon and two more MG 151s in the wing roots, and which incorporated a range of minor alterations compared to the D-9. It had been intended that the new D-12, which had an MK 108 mounted in the engine, and the D-13 would comprise up to 50 per cent of total production. They never did, and nor did the planned D-14, fitted with the Daimler-Benz DB 603 engine.

In 1944, as concerns grew about the possible appearance of the American B-29 Superfortress heavy bomber over Europe, so Kurt Tank began to develop another fighter that would emerge as the Ta 152. Based on the D-9, this high-altitude interceptor, with a longer fuselage than the D-9, did arrive with the Luftwaffe in limited numbers from January 1945, but the B-29 never came.

In Britain, while the Tempest V had given a good account of itself in operational service with the ADGB and 2nd TAF, the Tempest II was always seen as the favoured development. Fitted with the Centaurus engine, the Mk II had evolved from earlier

The last *Kommodore* of JG 51, Major Heinz Lange flew 'Yellow 10' from Flensburg in the first mock combat with a resident Tempest V. A Knight's Cross-holder and 73-victory ace, Lange had flown an astonishing 628 missions between September 1939 and May 1945. (EN-Archive)

The shape of things to come – newly delivered examples of Kurt Tank's Ta 152 high-altitude interceptors, assigned to 7./JG 301 at Alteno, Germany, in February 1945. In comparison with the American P-51D/K, the Ta 152 was found lacking in its initial rate of turn, but could then quickly tighten its turn to get behind a Mustang and bring its guns to bear. (EN-Archive)

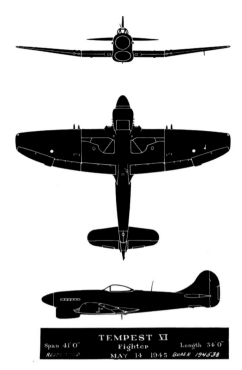

TEMPEST VI
Fighter
Span 41'0"   Length 34'0"
MAY 14 1945 BUAER 194638

plans for a Centaurus-powered Tornado. Intended for production by Gloster, the introduction of the radial-engined Mk II and the Sabre V-powered Mk VI was delayed because of that company's focus on the Meteor jet fighter. Nevertheless, two Tempest II prototypes were completed by early 1943 and the first flight was made on 28 June that year, the aircraft being powered by a rigidly-mounted Bristol Centaurus IV.

For production, it was intended that the Tempest II would have the same span as the V, but with a slightly longer fuselage, feature a tail unit similar in form to the V, short-barrelled Hispano Mk V cannon and a 2,520hp Centaurus V or VI engine. Performance was increased to a maximum speed of 442mph at 15,200ft. Just 50 such airframes were built by the Bristol Aircraft Company, while contracts for 900 Tempest IIs were placed with Hawker, which actually completed 402 examples.

The Mk V remained in service with the British Air Forces of Occupation in dwindling numbers until the last unit (No. 3 Sqn, which had also been the first equipped with the aircraft) converted to Vampires in mid-1948. The final operational Tempest left Germany in June of that year.

As the war in Europe drew to a close, work on the Mk II was still underway. Eventually examples saw service post-war, mainly in Germany (with Nos. 16, 26 and 33 Sqns) and India (Nos. 5, 20, 30 and 152 Sqns). The Sabre-powered Mk VI (of which 142 were built by Hawker) served with Nos. 6, 8, 39, 213 and 249 Sqns in the Middle East and Africa. As part of No. 324 Wing, Nos. 6 and 213 Sqns flew operations over Palestine in July 1947.

The last frontline unit to fly the Tempest operationally in the RAF was No. 33 Sqn based in Malaya, which flew its final sorties, with Mk IIs, from Butterworth in June 1951.

FURTHER READING

BOOKS

Avery, Max, with Shores, Christopher, *Spitfire Leader: The Story of Wing Cdr Evan 'Rosie' Mackie, DSO, DFC and Bar, DFC (US), Top Scoring RNZAF Fighter Ace* (Grub Street, London, 1997)

Bentley, Arthur, *Hawker Tempest* (Scale Models, February 1973)

Caldwell, Donald, *The JG 26 War Diary: Volume Two 1943-1945* (Grub Street, London, 1998)

Chacksfield, John, *Sir Sydney Camm: From Biplanes & 'Hurricanes' to 'Harriers'* (The Oakwood Press, Usk, 2010)

Crandall, Jerry, *The Focke-Wulf Fw 190 Dora – Volume One Fw 190 D-9* (Eagle Editions, Hamilton, 2007)

Crandall, Jerry, *The Focke-Wulf Fw 190 Dora – Volume Two Fw 190 D-9, D-11, D-13* (Eagle Editions, Hamilton, 2009)

Deboeck, Marc, Larger, Eric and Poruba, Tomás, *Focke-Wulf Fw 190D: Camouflage & Markings Part I* (JaPo, Hradec-Králové, 2005)

Deboeck, Marc, Larger, Eric and Poruba, Tomás, *Focke-Wulf Fw 190D: Camouflage & Markings Part II* (JaPo, Hradec-Králové, 2007)

Loo, Dr. P. E. van, *We Flew the Rocket Firing Typhoon, World War II Memories of No. 124 Wing RAF, Royal Netherlands Air Force History Unit* (The Hague, 1998)

Priller, Josef, *J.G.26 – Geschichte eines Jagdgeschwaders: Das J.G.26 (Schlageter) 1937–1945* (Motorbuch Verlag, Stuttgart, 1980)

Rodeike, Peter, *Focke-Wulf Jagdflugzeug – Fw 190 A, Fw 190 "Dora", Ta 152 H* (Struve-Druck, Eutin)

Shores, Christopher, and Thomas, Chris, *2nd Tactical Air Force: Volume Two – Breakout to Bodenplatte, July 1944 to January 1945* (Classic Publications, Hersham, 2005)

Shores, Christopher, and Thomas, Chris, *2nd Tactical Air Force: Volume Three – From the Rhine to Victory, January to May 1945* (Classic Publications, Hersham, 2006)

Shores, Christopher, and Thomas, Chris, *2nd Tactical Air Force: Volume Four – Squadrons, Camouflage and Markings, Weapons and Tactics 1943–1945* (Classic Publications, Hersham, 2008)

Shores, Christopher, & Williams, Clive, *Aces High – The Fighter Aces of the British and Commonwealth Air Forces in World War II* (Grub Street, London, 1994)

Smith, J. Richard, and Creek, Eddie J., *Focke-Wulf Fw 190 Volume Three 1944–1945* (Classic Publications, Hersham, 2013)

Thomas, Chris, *Osprey Combat Aircraft 117 – Tempest Squadrons of the RAF* (Osprey Publishing, Oxford, 2016)

Urbanke, Axel, *Green Hearts – First in Combat with the Dora 9* (Eagle Editions, Hamilton, 1998)

Wagner, Wolfgang, *Kurt Tank: Focke-Wulf's Designer and Test Pilot* (Schiffer Publishing, Atglen, 1998)

OTHER RESOURCES

Sir Sydney Camm Commemorative Society, *A Short History of Sir Sydney Camm CBE FRAes (1893–1966)* at www.sirsydneycamm.org/about-sir-sydney.html

HG Hawker Engineering Company, Hawker Aircraft Limited & Hawker Siddeley Aircraft at www.baesystems.com/en/heritage/hg-hawker

Jakl, Christian, *Oblt Hans Dortenmann – Flying Ace: His Aircraft and their History* at www.rlm.at/cont/gal23_e.htm

Napier Power Heritage Trust at www.npht.org/home/4577703109

National Archives, Kew, AIR50, Air Ministry: Combat Reports (various) via http://discovery.nationalarchives.gov.uk

The Hawker Tempest Page at www.hawkertempest.se

INDEX